By Christopher Dow

Fiction
Effigy
 Book I: Stroud
 Book II: Oakdale
The Books of Bob
 Devil of a Time
 Jumping Jehovah
The Clay Guthrie Mysteries
 The Dead Detective
 Landscape with Beast
 The Texas Troll Unlimited
 Darkness Insatiable
Roadkill
The Werewolf and Tide, and Other Compulsions

Nonfiction
Lord of the Loincloth (nonfiction novel)
Book of Curiosities: Adventures in the Paranormal
Occasional Pilgrimage: Essays on Film, Literature, and Other Matters
Living the Story: The Meandering Adventures of an Unknown Writer
 Vol.I: Growing Up Takes a Long Time
 Vol. II: Growing Old Takes Longer

Martial Arts
The Wellspring: An Inquiry into the Nature of Chi
Circling the Square: Observations on the Dynamics of Tai Chi Chuan
Elements of Power: Essays on the Art and Practice of Tai Chi Chuan
Alchemy of Breath: An Introduction to Chi Kung
Leaves on the Wind: A Survey of Martial Arts Literature (Vol. I–VI)

Poetry
City of Dreams
The Trip Out
Texas White Line Fever
Networks
A Dilapidation of Machinery
Puzzle Pieces: Selected Poems

Editor
The Abby Stone: The Poetry of Bartholo Dias
The Best of Phosphene
The Best of Dialog

Book of Curiosities

Book of Curiosities

Christopher Dow

Phosphene Publishing Company
Temple, Texas

Book of Curiosities
© 2014 by Christopher Dow
ISBN 13: 978-0-9851477-1-6
ISBN 10: 0985147717

Published by
Phosphene Publishing Company
Temple, Texas, U.S.A.
phosphenepublishing.com

Versions of the following articles have appeared elsewhere:

"Haunted: No. 10": *Fate*, June 1985.
"The Spirit of Bruja Canyon": *Fate*, January 1985.
"Smiley": *Fate*, August 2006.

For
Julie Dow
and
Charles Roberts

Contents

Book of Curiosities

Introduction: Queens of Egypt

IN 1981, A FRIEND OF mine, Charles Roberts, was a member of an archaeological expedition that was excavating a site at Nekhem, near the modern city of Idfu, in upper Egypt. Many of the excavators were American college students, and on one of their days off, they went to visit the nearby ruins of Heirakonopolis. Soon after they entered the ruins, an Egyptian man began following them. He tailed them for some time, holding back and peering at them around walls and between columns, making several of the students quite apprehensive.

At last, in front of the temple of Horus, he approached, waving a piece of paper. He asked if the students were Americans, and when they replied that they were, he told them he was the postmaster of Idfu and that he had been waiting for months for an American to visit his city. Presenting the paper he'd been waving, which was an envelope, he asked the students if it was a letter from America to America. If it was, would the students please see that it got to its proper destination? Amazed, the students saw that the letter had been mailed to an address in Queens, New York. The postmark read Brooklyn, New York, and was dated eight months earlier!

The letter was an example of something misplaced in space, but our reality also contains items and incidents that are equally misplaced in time or that, perhaps, come from some other dimension. If we could know with absolute certainty but one fact that is universally true and constant, we might use that fulcrum to lever our beings to a higher plane of understanding about the nature of both reality and the seemingly unreal. But despite the best efforts of theologians, philosophers, and scientists to parse and explicate reality, the universe is as mysterious today as it ever was. Humankind might think it knows what is going on, but tantalizing glimpses of non-ordinary reality occasionally pierce the veil of our perceptions, illustrating the limits of human knowledge and understanding and hinting at an underlying order, if not purpose, to the apparent randomness of creation.

The stories in this volume were not written as a coherent whole but as independent pieces, often years apart, and are grouped by category rather than chronologically. Most of the experiences they describe are ones in which I was a first-person observer or a direct participant. They frequently have left me in a position similar to that of the Idfu postmaster: disoriented and briefly holding something that might belong somewhere, but which is foreign to the limited realm of the here and now. They also have left me with the knowledge that a message, even if not completely understood, is a message nonetheless. And messages often come from far stranger places than Queens.

A Note on Names

Due to the nature of a few of the experiences related in this volume, a couple of the people involved did not want me to use their real names when I first issued this book. Often this was because of professional concerns, and I willingly obliged them with pseudonyms. However, they have since retired from employment and so have now given me permission to used their real names.

This edition also has undergone some editing and minor rewriting to make matters more accurate and more interesting.

Part I
Real and Unreal

Two Birds

"WHAT'S THAT?" MY WIFE, JULIE, asked.

It was a pleasant Saturday morning, and the windows were open. We were reading the newspaper and drinking coffee in the living room when something dark and fist-sized hopped along the inner window sill in the dining room.

It was a bird, and a second bird followed the first onto the sill. The exterior sill of that particular window was rotted, and the screen hung askew at the bottom, permitting the birds to edge inside. I'd been meaning to fix the sill but hadn't gotten around to it.

"What are we going to do?" Julie asked.

I got up and slowly approached the window, hoping to frighten the birds into leaving the way they'd entered. The second one saw me coming and scrambled back out through the crack, but the first panicked and began fluttering around the dining room. I quickly shut the doors to the kitchen and hall, then I propped open the front screen door. After a short chase, the bird saw the open door, dashed through, and was gone.

I shut the screen door and returned to the paper and coffee.

"Doesn't that mean something?" Julie asked.

I knew she would.

"I don't know," I replied, pretending to concentrate on the paper. But in truth, I was a little curious myself.

"I know it means something," she insisted. "I remember Aunt Teet saying something about it. Don't you have a dictionary of superstitions?"

Julie, coming from an African American background, was more in touch with superstition than I was. Her grandmother, Minon, and her great aunt, Teet, were from a Louisiana of, now, a century ago and were steeped in the lore of former African slaves who peopled the wetlands of the upper Gulf Coast. If your right hand itches, you're going to get money; if your left hand itches, you're going to lose some. If someone sweeps you with a broom, you're going to jail. If your right eye twitches, you're going....

You see what I mean. As for me, I never thought that some prohibitions—against letting black cats cross your path or walking under ladders—were anything more than reflections of prescientific ignorance. Others I'd always chalked up to practical considerations—the fear of spilling salt, for example. I figured that was a holdover from Medieval times when salt was a valuable commodity, and parents, as parents will, used a scare tactic to keep their kids from being carelessly wasteful of it, and that scare tactic became gospel.

But some old wives' tales, I knew, did contain a grain of truth, such as rubbing moldy bread into a cut to help cure it. As we know now, bread mold contains penicillin. So, while I was open to a validity behind some superstitions, a wild bird in the house being a harbinger of some sort seemed more along the lines of black cats and ladders rather than of bread-mold cures.

"Okay," I said. "I'll look it up."

I went to my study, found *The Giant Book of Superstitions* by Claudia de Lys (Citadel Press, 1979), and read, "To the superstitious-minded, if a bird flies into the house, or taps at a window, it is a bad omen; auguring death within the year to someone living in the house." Indeed, as J.E. Cirlot points out in *A Dictionary of Symbols* (Philosophical Library, 1962), birds have long been associated with the souls of the dead. Although the superstition extends to all birds—even pictures of birds—the core of it concerns wild rather than pet birds entering a domicile.

But I sure as heck wasn't going to tell Julie I'd read that the birds were an omen of death visiting our house. I returned to the living room, and said, "It didn't say much."

"Let me see."

I had no choice but to fetch the superstition book. She read the entry then said, "I knew it was bad."

I tried to seem nonchalant as I finished the paper and my coffee. Soon after, I dressed and left the house to run some errands. When I returned a couple of hours later, Julie had an interesting story to tell.

At the time, Julie was a vet technician working for a local veterinarian. A day or so earlier, a couple had brought in a Rottweiler that had been shot. The shooting was an accident, the man said. The couple left the dog but hadn't been back, and the dog was still recuperating at the clinic.

This much I already knew since Julie had mentioned it as an interesting story the evening after the dog had been brought in. But now the story had gotten even more interesting.

About twenty minutes after I left to run my errands, a knock sounded on the door. Julie answered it to discover two plainclothes Houston homicide detectives on the porch. They wanted to ask her a few questions.

Julie agreed to talk to them and invited them in. One stepped into the house, but the other remained on the porch during the conversation. They wanted to know about the dog with the gunshot wound and the people who'd brought it in.

It seemed that the dog belonged to the husband of the woman who'd brought in the dog, but the man who'd been with her was not her husband. The husband had been found dead, murdered by gunshot on the same day the dog was admitted to the clinic. Apparently, the woman and/or the man had murdered the husband and accidentally shot the dog at the same time —or maybe shot it because it was defending its owner.

Julie told the detectives what she could, and they left.

I'm sure you've noticed the correspondence: Wild birds entering a domicile are harbingers of death. Two wild birds enter our house, and one comes in briefly, while the other merely hovers about the sill. Half an hour later, two homicide detectives investigating a murder pay a visit, and one comes in briefly, while the other merely hovers on the porch. Incidentally, the window the birds entered was only about eight feet from the front door.

Make of it what you will. I still don't worry about spilled salt, black cats, or ladders—unless there's a can of paint at the top. But penicillin has served me well on occasion. And birds—well, I can't prove a thing, but the coincidence is striking.

Fire in the Sky

MY FRIENDS—CHARLES AND MIKE—and I were nearing the end of a weeklong trip to Big Bend National Park in West Texas. We had just come Charles and my second visit and Mike's first to Bruja Canyon, which are discussed elsewhere in this book.

Charles and I knew of a spot where we wanted to camp. It lay just off the Old Maverick Road, which runs through the desert on the west side of the park. Charles and I had driven this road on earlier trips, but we'd never stopped. The western boundary of the park is just a few miles away, and about fifteen miles beyond that is an upland topped by three principal mountain: Black Mesa, the Solitario, and Aqua Fria Mountain.

The place where we wanted to camp was along the east side of the road's southern stretch. There, etched into the Earth's skin, is a maze of deep gullies, arroyos, and washes that are interesting to see. Charles and I always wanted a closer look, and now was an opportune time. It turned out to be a lucky choice for a camping spot.

After we found a place where the gullies and wash-es were close to the road, we parked, got our gear, and scrambled down into the maze. We didn't go far before we located a fairly level place to set up camp. After we had, we spent a couple of hours exploring the warren of gullies and washes, then as the afternoon waned, we returned to camp to eat.

By then, the sun had gone down, followed by the inevitable half-hour of wind that sucked into the cool-ing darkness as the desert heat bled into the night. Af-ter the wind died, the air was pleasantly cool beneath a clear, spangled sky. We lay on our sleeping bags, con-templating the stars and talking about our trip. Our conversation finally wound down, and we were settling in for sleep when suddenly a meteor fell from the sky.

This was no simple shooting star streaking silently and briefly across the constellations. It was very large, and it fell straight down directly to the west of us. The sky lit up almost as brightly as daytime, and a tremen-dous roaring, hissing whoosh split the air. The remains of the meteor must have been of some size because it struck the ground with a fairly loud boom. Since we were down in the arroyos, we couldn't see exactly where the impact occurred, but from the dull sound of it and the fact that we felt no shock from the im-pact, it was many miles away.

We briefly discussed trying to find the impact site, but we had to abandon the idea. The impact had hap-pened somewhere in an area of about two hundred square miles of rugged terrain, and we were simply not prepared or equipped to undertake the kind of search that would be required to locate the site. It probably was on private ranch land, anyway. Also, the meteor's fall must have been witnessed by residents of the town of Study Butte, which was less than ten miles to our northwest. They undoubtedly knew the terrain better than we did and would find the crater more easily than we could.

So, the next morning, we packed up, hiked out of the arroyos to the truck, and headed on to our final campsite before heading back to Houston, carrying with us our memories of that fire in the sky.

Nail

IN 2010, MY WIFE, JULIE, and I decided to spend our spring vacation exploring New Mexico. The state is billed as the "Land of Enchantment," and it is certainly that. We had a truly fantastic trip. I'd driven across the state a few times in my younger years and stopped at a couple of places, but I hadn't spent much time in it. Julie had only driven through when we'd gone to Grand Tetons and Yellowstone National Parks. We were excited, and I plotted our route to take in as many of New Mexico's natural and human-made wonders as possible.

One of our stops was to be Chaco Canyon, center of the Anasazi Culture, which had unraveled by about 1200 BC. I'd been there once before and had been struck by the site's profound character. I wanted Julie to experience it, and I also wanted to see if the deeply mysterious way I'd felt about it on my first visit there would still be the same.

There are two roads into the site. Both are dirt, one roughly from the northeast and one roughly from the southwest. On my first visit, I'd come in on the northeast road, and I remembered it as being rough and often washboarded but entirely passable, even to passenger cars and campers. This time, Julie and I would be coming in from the other direction, and I assumed that the road would be very much the same, though it was a bit longer in length—thirty-five miles or so. I had no fear of the terrain since the road was well maintained, plus, we were driving my Xterra, which had four-wheel drive in the event of an unexpectedly rough situation.

I generally love to drive across deserts on dirt roads, but this time, despite my semi-familiarity with the terrain, careful planning, and tough vehicle, an odd and unsettling idea began to creep into my thoughts every time I contemplated driving across the desert on this road. I'm not one to experience paranoia when driving, even in out-of-the-way places, but I couldn't shake this particular idea—a sort of visualization, really.

It began about two weeks before our departure: In my mind, I kept seeing a flat tire with a huge nail—something like ten inches long—embedded in it. At first, I passed it off. After all, how could anyone get a huge nail in their tire driving a dirt road in the desert? But the more I experienced this visualization, the more worried I became, and my imagination took over. Was it a premonition that some nefarious person would lay a trap for an unwary motorist in a desolate location? It wasn't a question I could answer, but I was disturbed by frequent recurrences of the vision of the huge nail embedded in the flat tire.

Not wanting to make Julie nervous, I didn't mention the vision to her, and I eventually pushed down thoughts about it as our departure approached. After we were off, I forgot about it entirely. We eventually worked our way to Gallup, where we spent the night. The next morning, we headed toward the dirt road that would take us to Chaco Canyon.

As we approached the intersection of the blacktop and the dirt road, my unsettling thought of the huge nail in the flat tire resurfaced, but I ignored it as I steered onto the dirt road. A mile or so down the road, we passed a ranch house that sat about a quarter of a mile away. Next to the entrance to the ranch house's dirt driveway was a small table of plywood weathered a silver gray that had a number of pieces of handmade turquoise jewelry on it, small price tags fluttering at the ends of thin strings. A sign proclaimed that anyone who wanted to buy some of the jewelry could take what they wanted and leave the money in the jar on the table. Julie wanted to stop, so we did, and she chose a pair of turquoise earrings and paid the jar. We got back into the car and drove on down the road.

This section of the road was in very good condition, but I started wondering about the nail. Where would such a thing come from out here in the middle of nowhere? I realized pretty quickly that it could come from one of the cattle guards that we had to cross every time we came to a fence line, though the nail's size seemed out of proportion to a construction such as a cattle guard. Maybe they used big nails to fasten the large creosoted timbers supporting the cattle guard to each other or to the hard, rocky ground.

About ten miles in, we came over a rise to see a long straight stretch of road ahead of us, and about half a mile down this stretch sat a car with two people standing outside of it. As we neared, we could tell that it was the bumper-sticker festooned car we'd frequently seen the day before. The taller of the two women waved her arms to flag us down. I slowed to a stop and rolled down my window. They had a flat tire, she told me. She had a spare, but she couldn't remove the damaged tire because the lug nuts were frozen. Would I be so kind as to inform the rangers at Chaco Canyon so they could send someone to change the tire?

Nonsense, I told her, and I pulled up about fifty feet and parked. I got out and went back to the women's car. The lug nuts were very tight, but I stood on the lug wrench and bounced to loosen them. As I jacked up the car, the woman said she hadn't thought of loosening them like that. When the car was high enough, I twiddled off the nuts, pulled the tire off, and looked at it to see what had caused the flat.

Embedded in it was a ten-inch nail.

The woman marveled that she'd driven over such a thing out here in the desert, and I mentioned that it might have come from one of the cattle guards. I put on her spare and showed her the proper way to tighten the lug nuts. After I put the flat in her trunk, she and her companion thanked me, and while they got their belongings together, Julie and I drove on to Chaco Canyon.

Chaco Canyon

TUCKED IN THE BROAD, DRY valley of Chaco Canyon in northwest New Mexico, a civilization flourished for centuries. Its architects built their structures to last, with intricate and refined stone walls that both sheltered and aligned along mystic currents dictated by the paths of the sun and moon across the greater desert of stars. Though we do not know exactly who these people were or why they built these buildings as they did, the monuments show that their builders thought and planned for some future.

But what was it they thought? For what future did they plan? We probably will never know, but we do know some of the sounds they made. There were cries of infants and wheezes of infirmity, howls of triumph and screams of pain, moans of lovers and sighs of loneliness, babbles of anticipation and hushes of excitement.

Then, suddenly, it was over. The people of Chaco Canyon, it seems, just vanished, leaving only their stone buildings littering the landscape like the exposed skeletons of unknown creatures huge enough to have shaken the earth but fragile enough to have passed forever. This durable monument was the future they'd built for. And though the buildings are decaying imperceptibly beneath the sandy fingers of desert winds, many of them still stand strong, even after a millennium of neglect.

And there is something else about the buildings that is as durable as the adamancy of their stone. It is their strangeness. It speaks in a voice too hushed to comprehend about the mysteries of the culture that erected these complexes—a strangeness that has transcended and outlasted the culture. Even in the bright sunlight, the buildings are dark, brooding, and somber, and the meticulously ordered walls hide mazes of passageways and rooms that seem as much like prison cells as habitat—passages and rooms where even the lost find no answers.

Where are those who lived here—the people who rose from nowhere to create this maze that yet puzzles before returning to whence they came? Probably their remnants spread outward to build, in progressive declensions of space, time, and sophistication, the cliff dwellings of Mesa Verde and the adobe structures of the American Southwest.

But if the people themselves have gone, their spirits remain. I have seen them in the nearby dark, sheer, barren rock hills that rise like eidetic shoals from dusty seas of desert's forgetfulness. Etched in those rocks is a multitude of pareidolial faces, jumbled and often weird and haunted. Nature alone could not have created this massively anthropomorphic landscape. The winds and cutting sands that carved it could only have been channeled by the ghosts of the architects whose exodus left arcane ruins lying lifeless, forgotten, and alone in their broad, dry valley.

Frankie the Vampire

VAMPIRES, ONCE RELEGATED TO THE folklore of superstitious peoples, have risen in stature to become icons of popular culture. Today, hardly anyone could fail to know about these undead bloodsuckers. Indeed, a whole vampire fashion cult has emerged whose devotees emulate vampires—they dress in costume and wear false fangs, and the more outrély dedicated are so faithful they even drink human blood. Put them in the sun, though, and all that happens is they get skin cancers like everybody else.

But while there are a lot of pretenders, that doesn't mean that there aren't real vampires out there. Or at least some folks who sure seem like they might be. Take Frankie, for instance.

I'm not calling him Frankie to be facetious. Stephen and Dana said that was his name, and they should know because they rented rooms from him not long after they graduated from college. Stephen couldn't recall Frankie's last name, and Dana said he never knew it. Later, for a short time in the mid 1970s, I shared an apartment with

Dana, and Stephen was part of our circle of friends, and they told me the story.

Looking for an inexpensive place to live, Stephen and Dana responded to an ad in the newspaper that offered a house-sharing arrangement. They called the phone number, and the voice that answered said to come by after 9 pm. There was nothing particularly unusual about the house; it wasn't a spooky old mansion, just a regular house in the Montrose area of Houston, built some time between the world wars.

Frankie met them at the door at the appointed hour. He was dark haired, of average height, and slenderly built, with an almost gaunt face. And he was very pale. He invited them in and showed them the house. The arrangements were simple. He would rent them most of the house except for his own apartment, or series of rooms, which occupied one end of the house. As he had his own bath and kitchen facilities in his apartment, the main kitchen, bathroom, living room, and two bedrooms, all completely furnished, would be for Stephen and Dana's exclusive use.

Frankie told them that they probably wouldn't see much of him because he worked nights at a blood bank and slept during the day. As Stephen had just graduated from anesthesiology school, Frankie's employment didn't seem outrageous, even if it was unusual.

The arrangements were ideal, and the rent was reasonable, so Stephen and Dana moved in. True to his word, Frankie remained, for the most part, unseen and unheard. About the only time they ever saw him was when they paid their rent, in cash, as per Frankie's request. If they knocked on Frankie's door and he did answer, which was a rarity, he would come to the door and open it to speak to them, but after the night they first met him, he never crossed the threshold into their area of the house. And he never came to the door or answered their knocks during the daytime.

Frankie's door was always locked, and Stephen and Dana never once saw him enter or leave his rooms. This was decidedly odd. After all, Frankie claimed to have a job, which would mean he had to leave the house at least occasionally. In the beginning, though often either Stephen or Dana was home, they never saw him leave, which they definitely should have since the front door was off their living room and the sole back door exited from their kitchen. If Frankie was leaving, it was through a window.

Not long after they moved in, Stephen and Dana began to have eerie feelings of being watched at night, even when the blinds were down and the shades drawn. A pall of oppression seemed to settle over the house, and they had difficulty sleeping. Over several months, the situation grew more uncomfortable, and their unspecified anxiety graduated to apprehension and then fear. They began to avoid the house as much as possible at night, though in the daytime it wasn't as bad, for in the light, the gloom seemed somewhat dispelled.

As the oppression deepened, Stephen and Dana couldn't help but discuss the house's unpleasant atmosphere and their growing fear. In particular, they considered Frankie's appearance, his mysterious and apparently nocturnal habits, and most of all, his supposed employment. Although there was never any hard evidence that Frankie was a vampire, the gestalt seemed a little too close for comfort.

After about six months, they hurriedly moved out—during the day—foregoing their security deposit and deliberately failing to bid pale, gaunt Frankie adieu.

Chinese Oracles

THROUGHOUT THE AGES, HUMANS have developed many ways to interface with mysterious sources of wisdom. What any given individual might think of these sources—astrology, the Tarot, scrying, trance mediumship, casting bones, and so forth—probably depends on his or her personal experience with any given method and insights gained from those experiences. The question remains, however: Do these techniques actually result in valid communications, or is any information derived from them automatically suspect? The answer, in the short term, might rest on the validity of any given source. A bogus medium will give bogus information, and there certainly are bogus mediums as well as self-deluded ones.

But are all such sources necessarily fraudulent, false, or otherwise spurious as the confirmed skeptic would have us believe? I can't answer that question for anyone but myself, but I have found that such sources can provide tremendous insights into the events, meanings, and direction of my life. Several incidents concerning otherworldly sources of information are related elsewhere in this book, but here, I'd like to tell about two relatively minor though somewhat telling incidences that have bolstered my belief that esoteric communications techniques can, in fact, produce genuine messages. Both con- cern two principal methods developed by the Chinese: the *I Ching* and Chinese astrology.

Since my early twenties, I've frequently consulted the *I Ching*. I prefer the Cary F. Baynes English rendering of Richard Wilhelm's German translation from the original Chinese work (Bollingen/Princeton University Press, 1950). There's something about a translation of an oracle that is introduced by Carl Jung, himself a believer in a universal, if unconscious, source of ultimate wisdom, that lends this particular version more credence to me than some of its more pop or New Age successors.

When I first started consulting the *I Ching* by casting the coins—my preferred method—I was mildly skeptical but also curious and willing to give the oracle the benefit of the doubt in order to see if it might impart anything of value. For a couple of years, my castings and the resulting answers were promising but also often ambiguous. Sometimes the answer seemed right on, and at other times, completely off the mark. Then came one decisive moment when I finally believed.

The question I asked the oracle on this occasion is not important here. Suffice it to say that I asked the question and threw the coins. But when I read the hexagram that was revealed, which had no moving lines, I did not like the answer, or also possible, I did not want to ac- knowledge the truth of it. So I asked the question again and cast the coins. The resulting hexagram was exactly the same as the first, again with no moving lines.

Frustrated, I put away the book and coins and pondered the answer. I still did not like it, so the next day, I asked the same question and threw the coins again. This time, the resulting hexagram was different than the one revealed the day before. Finally, I thought, I'm getting the real answer—the answer I wanted. I excitedly turned to the new statement from the oracle, which was Hexagram 4, somewhat disturbingly titled: Ming/Youthful Folly. The Judgment, which is a hexagram's initial statement, read:

> Youthful folly has success.
> It is not I who seek the young fool;
> The young fool seeks me.
> At the first oracle I inform him.
> If he asks two or three times, it is importunity.
> If he importunes, I give him no information.
> Perseverance furthers.

The text basically said, "I already told you the answer twice, you young fool. Don't ask again."

This exchange taught me to give the *I Ching* oracle some credence. This is not the place for a primer on how to calculate a hexagram from coin tosses. For that, you should consult the *I Ching* itself. But throwing two identical hexagrams twice in a row to the same question is statistically unlikely, and the lack of moving lines in both casts also is statistically significant because it meant that the configuration of heads and tails on each toss was exactly the same in both cases and without either triple heads or triple tails, either of which result in moving lines.

Then, to have added on top of that statistical un- likelihood a statement—or tone, if you will—of dis- gruntlement from the oracle on the third throw both lent the *I Ching* personality and gave a sense that even an oracle can be irritated by trivial requests or disregard of the in- formation it imparts. The exchange also taught me to try to understand—or at least accept— any given casting with grace rather than badgering. If I don't understand, perhaps that merely highlights my limitations. In fact, disbelief in a given answer often indicates resistance.

*   *   *

Now I'll tell you about the blue pig. My sister, Shan- non, noted it when she came for a visit, and we were driving around, looking at the city.

The blue pig's history is brief but interesting. Some years ago—around the year 2000, my wife gave me a copy of my Chinese horoscope, as she does every year. I have always found the Chinese horoscope as illuminating with regard to my personality as its Western counterpart.

Among other things, the book said that my lucky charm for the upcoming year would be a blue colored, pig-shaped key-chain fob. I read this and completely dismissed it. For one thing, I don't particularly like key- chain fobs. I have enough keys weighing down my pocket without adding to their bulk a useless ornament that no one ever sees. This was in the days before most cars had remote key locks, but at least these sorts of fobs have a purpose. Also, I have never been much of a believer in lucky charms, so my eyes moved over the recommendation without my brain doing more than scanning the information.

The next morning, I drove in to work at my accustomed early hour. I was always the first person to arrive at the office by a margin of well over an hour, mostly because I could either get some serious work done during the quiet before everyone else arrived or surf the Internet without distractions. Just before I'd left work the afternoon before, I'd checked my mail box and taken out everything that was in it. And the first thing I did in the morning—after I'd gotten a pot of coffee brewing—was to check the box again to see if anything had come after I'd left the day before.

On this particular morning, something had. Sitting in my box, all by itself, was a blue-colored, pig-shaped key-chain fob.

I was astounded, but my brain immediately started working over the possibilities of who might have put it there. The list was one person long. Most of the twenty or so people in the office had no interest in or understanding of the esoteric and probably didn't know much about the recommendations of Chinese astrology or would have singled me out for a demonstration of their knowledge. The one exception was our IT tech, who was gay and second- generation Vietnamese. Out of everyone in the office, he was most likely to know about Chinese astrology. As soon as I had the opportunity, I asked him if he'd put the blue pig in my mail box, but he said he hadn't. I don't know if he was telling the truth, but he had no reason to lie.

Whether he was telling the truth or not, the timing of the key fob's appearance with my reading of the recommendation the night before, which the IT tech could not possibly have known about, was particularly synchronistic. I fastened the fob to my key chain and carried it throughout the year and for a couple of more.

Did the blue pig bring me luck? Who knows? That year doesn't stand out in my memory as particularly no- table with regard to luck, but I guess it could have been a whole lot worse, so maybe the blue pig at least did what it could to make matters stay on an even keel.

My sister was introduced because these days the blue pig hangs from my rearview mirror. I now have a differ- ent car with a remote lock fob, so the pig just didn't fit in my pocket any more. But I couldn't part with him, either. I hung him facing forward as I drive, so he can get a de- cent view and see ahead of me, just in case.

Does he bring me luck? Who can say?

In the Stream

SOMETIMES WHEN I'M FEELING RESTLESS, I'll go for a drive. Occasionally, I'll cruise around the city, but I experience Houston traffic every day, and I'd rather drive in the country. That doesn't leave many options. Houston is large enough that it can take an hour or more to traverse the city, so, from where I live, the only practical directions are east and south. I like to go east, toward the coast and around Galveston Bay, but the coastal prairie south of Houston has a lot of winding small roads and several points of interest.

One spring day in 2002, I got in my car and headed for TX 288, the freeway that runs south out of the city and winds up at the Gulf Coast in the Freeport/Lake Jackson area. I could drive all the way to Freeport during an extended jaunt, but the point is not necessarily to drive far or fast but to relax and see something different and peaceful. I'll usually drive out 288 far enough to get out of the city then, taking side roads, zigzag back and forth across the countryside, checking out the scenery.

On this particular day, I'd been driving for about an hour and had just zagged back onto 288 from the east. As I drove farther south, I kept an eye out for a likely looking side road to the west. A few miles later, I spotted one and took it. Half a mile or so down this country blacktop, I noticed a well-maintained gravel and dirt road that intersected to the right and, prompted by curiosity, turned onto it. The dirt road was in good shape, but I drove slowly, savoring the temporary freedom, the aloneness, and the plume of dust spinning off my tires.

I proceeded about a mile until the dirt road crossed a creek. Country streams are fascinating, not the least for what locals throw into them, so I decided to stop and take a look. I figured I'd see some old furniture, maybe an appliance or two, and some unidentifiable machine parts. I parked about fifty feet beyond the bridge, got out, and walked back.

The air was warm, stagnant, heavy, and laced with an odor of organic decay that was strong and unpleasant but not overpowering. The bridge was a simple beam construction without guard rails, and I walked right up to the middle on the east, upstream side. I was still six or eight feet from the edge when I saw something in the streambed that made me jerk back and gasp.

The narrow watercourse was eight feet below me, and the ugly, murky water was choked with algae that was a dirty chartreuse. There were a few of the requisite unidentifiable mechanical parts and an old and rotting stuffed chair, but that wasn't what had shocked me. Lying there on the left bank, almost in the water, was the body of a horse.

It was a male, black in color, and it was lying on its left side, it's feet toward me. It wasn't particularly large, but it's smooth, well-defined muscles implied that it had been strong, and it didn't appear to have been decrepit or infirm in any way. The body wasn't yet bloated, so it couldn't have been there more than a few hours, though blowflies were beginning to cluster on it.

It was headless.

I stood and stared, stunned and taking in the fact that the powerful, black-maned neck ended in nothing. At last, I began to look for other details, noting that no head lay nearby And there was no massive splash of blood, as would certainly have been present had the horse been decapitated where I found it. Nor were there any footprints in the mud around the body, further indicating that the decapitation had occurred prior to the body being pushed off the bridge. The cut itself was very clean. Probably the horse had been killed and decapitated elsewhere before being dumped in the creek the preceding night or possibly that very morning.

I may have been analyzing, but I wasn't really thinking. Instead, I felt a combined sense of shock and wonder tinged with a touch of horror. How...why had this come to be? At last, I looked away from the horse to its surroundings, as if the streambed might provide some answers. There on the other side of the stream, half-embedded in muck, was a cow skull.

I realized then, looking around further, that the rest of the cow's remains—mostly bone and gristle and a tatter of hide—lay scattered about the right bank and in the water.

Two carcasses—one many months if not a year or more old, the other so recent I could taste the dust of the vehicle that had carried it here.

A detached cow femur pointed beneath the bridge. Certainly more of the cow was under my feet and on the west side of the bridge. I crossed, not sure what I'd find but knowing it probably would be more of the cow.

It was hard to tell if more of the cow had indeed washed under the bridge because the streambed on the west side held five large animal carcasses in various stages of decomposition. None were as recent as the horse. The most complete was a cow, well up on the left bank: a ragged shell of hide stretched over a cage of bone from which the bird of life had long since fled.

The rest ranged from a totally collapsed version of the cow to several large grease spots decorated with bone and mats of skin and hair. One of these was large enough to have been a cow, but the others seemed much too small and the hair wrong. I suppose they could have been calves or ponies, but it was just as likely that they'd been goats, pigs, or even large dogs. Whatever they were, they'd been there a long time, and no skulls remained to aid identification.

The air was more tainted on this side of the bridge, and there were more flies in the air. I looked at the nasty water as it meandered off in its gully along the edge of an adjacent field and decided that burying such large carcasses must be too great a chore, so the erstwhile owners simply maneuvered them onto a truck, drove them out here, and shoved them off, over the edge. And from the look of things, it was a regular habit with the locals, though it occurred to me that half an hour with a backhoe in a field would be more sanitary and safer for the environment. After all, this creek was probably contaminated now for miles downstream. But then, backhoes cost money, and the anonymous streambed was quick, easy, and cheap.

Ten minutes of examining this sylvan charnel pit was all I could take. I returned to my car and resumed my drive. Soon after, the dirt road ended at a paved road, and a couple of miles down this, I crossed a bridge over another, larger, stream, fed in part by the charnel creek I'd just seen. As I did, I couldn't help but wonder, with a touch of paranoia, if large animal carcasses rotted on the banks below, just out of sight of passing motorists. I've seen a lot of local creeks, and though people seem to have a penchant for throwing all manner of trash and refuse into the waterways that nourish the earth, I'd never seen anything like this. But then, the carcasses will eventually deteriorate and add nutrients to the stream, while the metal debris and furniture won't.

The real puzzles, though, were the horse's apparent health and, most of all, its missing head. The other carcasses that were identifiable still retained their heads, or at least their skulls. Why was the horse different? And the cut was very clean. What instrument or tool could do that? Perhaps the skull was a marketable commodity. I'm sure I'll never know.

Part II
Shadows

Looking Back, Looking Forward

LIFE IS FULL OF MYSTERIES, not the least of which are what came before we were born and what happens after we die. The pure materialist says we come from nothing and return there. Some religious thought holds that we come, essentially, from nothing, and that we're going to a just reward, either Heaven or Hell. The predominant alternate view is that we originally come from some source—the Tao, the Great Spirit, God, etc.—that we've lived many lives before this, and that we'll live many after in an attempt to perfect ourselves enough to return to the source.

The materialist's stance seems to me to be untenable to anyone but a materialist. Materialists often ignore or discount the great number of reports of paranormal and mystical experiences, often from reliable witnesses, many of whom form the foundations of our culture, citing lack of empirical evidence and pronouncing that, in any case, paranormal events are impossible because they violate the laws of science. But science itself is full of instances of truths we now hold as self-evident, proven, or detected that once were dismissed as superstitious nonsense or outlandish fantasy and falsehood—or not thought about at all. And not only was much of what science now holds true totally unthinkable a century ago, much of what it held true then is now known to be false.

Just because we haven't discovered methods or developed instruments to detect spiritual energies that are neither created by birth nor destroyed by death doesn't mean they don't exist. The truth is, they do. After all, even science itself holds that energy can neither be created nor destroyed, and certainly life is some sort of energy that animates the body in life and vacates it upon death. And there *is* an instrument sensitive enough to detect it: a living being. Finally, consensus opinion—which is notoriously unscientific—would hold that love and hate are as real as the chair you are sitting on, yet they cannot be quantified or measured by instruments.

A materialist might argue that spiritual energy is a far cry from love or hate, but is it? Almost anyone would admit that they can "feel" another's anger or compassion or love. If I can feel the emotions of another person, then there must be some sort of energetic connection between us. This implies both a broadcast and reception system as well as a medium through which such interactions can occur. It also means that our life forces must extend beyond our bodies and interact in subtle ways. This, in itself, affirms the existence of a field of life energy that surrounds each of us, that can be colored by emotion, and that can potentially affect or be affected by a wide spectrum of energies.

True, such an energy field need not be connected to a godhead. It could simply be a by-product of having a nervous system that generates bioelectricity and attendant bioelectromagnetic fields, without recourse to an external creator. However, animal bodies—and some other sorts of bodies, such as stars and planets—generate magnetic and gravitational fields, and those fields all overlap, so certainly we are all constantly connected by ever-expanding and complexly interacting forces and waves of energy. Reality is, perhaps, created by the manifold interactions of all the ripples animating the base quantum substance of reality—the universal chi—but we still have to grapple with what that substance is and what causes the ripples.

Such a medium, and transmission method still do not require a supreme being or motivator, but it is interesting that through ripples of energy, we have awareness of ourselves, of each other, and often, of something larger even than all the waveforms populating reality. It is this awareness that is important. Awareness implies a watcher, and a nonphysical watcher seated within the physical construct of a vibration-based reality is one way of defining a spiritual energy—a soul, if you will—that is present in the living and that, because energy cannot be created or destroyed, goes elsewhere after the body ceases to anchor it to the here-and-now.

The conventional religious stance also seems to me to be too limiting. In it, our just reward is either Heaven or Hell, but can many of us meager humans lead the truly exemplary life that might justify eternal reward in a merit-based Heaven? I don't know about you, but for me, it can take a lot of practice to get something right, and I think that is especially true for leading an exemplary life. The idea that faith, alone, is sufficient to send you to Heaven, might populate Heaven with those who were faithful but who also behaved heinously toward their fellow humans here on Earth. In the end, I think Hell would overflow before Heaven had more than a scattered population that might be made up of moral cretins.

I'm drawn to the third view, popularly known as reincarnation. It accepts spiritual energies, and it gives us poor, limited humans a chance to perfect ourselves and truly deserve a return to oneness with the Tao or God. The following story might not provide convincing evidence for reincarnation, but it is illustrative of the point.

In the early 1980s, I knew a woman named Margie Kerr. She was a trained hypnotherapist, and I met her when she began taking tai chi chuan lessons from me. During part of the year that I instructed her, she was just getting her hypnotherapy practice off the ground, and she didn't have any money to spare, so I quit charging her for lessons. As a form of trade, she offered to hypnotize me and lead me through a past life regression.

On the appointed day, I lay back in the recliner chair in her hypnotherapy room, Margie did her work, and I let myself relax and respond. In a few moments, I was under. During the entire experience, I was completely conscious of being myself, but that consciousness was concentrated within me, and I had virtually no awareness of my body. It was much like being deeply asleep, then waking, clear of mind but not yet connected to my body.

Margie suggested I look back into my spirit's history to see if I could become aware of one of my past personalities. Nothing happened for some time, but then I began to "awake" in another body. The experience was different than waking in my own body. In this other body, I had no volition—I was merely a passenger who could see, hear, and feel, to a partial extent, the sensations of this other body but who had absolutely no control. At the same time, I also could sense the thoughts and emotions of this other person without being able to read them literally. Think of watching a foreign film without subtitles or knowing the language—you can basically tell what's going on and the tenor of the emotional content, though the details and specifics might be lost.

The process of waking was not as if emerging from sleep, either, because the person into which I awoke was not sleeping but sitting in a tiny hut, repairing a piece of rude clothing. Instead, it was as if a shadowy mist dissipated from in front of me, starting in the center, permitting me to see through this other man's eyes. First, I became aware that I was in another person, and then I could see his chest, then his hands sewing the cloth, then his lap, knees, feet, and peripherally, the crude chair he was sitting on. Gradually, some of the interior of the hovel in which he lived was revealed. The hut was lit by low flames in a small stone hearth and a single smoky candle or grease lamp.

The person I was inside of was not me as I am, yet, oddly, I could tell it was a version of me, with some of the same character traits. He did not seem to be aware of my presence.

Margie asked me to describe the person I was in and his environment. This was somewhat difficult to do since I could only describe what I could see, and my host was mostly looking at his sewing work.

Though I could not see his face or head, I was aware of his self-image. He was white, somewhere between thirty and forty years old, of medium height, and very slender. I had the impression that he was fairly plain of features and that his hair was roughly block-cut, tangled but not especially dirty or matted, and a mousy brown in color. The clothing I could see was all simple and handmade out of rough cloth and animal skins held together with wide, crude leather stitching.

The hut was very small, roughly oval, and only about eight or ten feet on the long axis. It was constructed of logs, sticks, and one wall of packed earth. The small hearth occupied the earthen side of the hut, and the interior was cozy, dry, and warm. Niches and shelves here and there on the walls held the grease lamp and the man's simple possessions. One of the items, hanging from the low ceiling, was a small cage built of sticks, inside of which was some sort of small animal. I could see the animal's movements out of the corner of my host's eyes, but because he never looked directly at the cage, I couldn't tell if it was a bird or a small furry animal like a chipmunk.

My host felt a great sense of security and contentment in his cozy home. I had the sense it was well concealed in the forest, perhaps nestled in the hollow left when a huge tree had fallen and its rootball had ripped out of the ground. That would account for the one wall of packed earth.

I described my surroundings to Margie, but I could not read much from my host aside from his general feeling of contentment and the fact that he led a simple life. He was an illiterate peasant with no sense of history or culture and without much thought beyond his immediate needs and limited life experience.

As nothing much seemed to be happening except for repair of the item of clothing, Margie suggested I shift my perspective slightly to take in another moment in this same person's time line. I did, and this time there was nothing gradual about my awakening. It was quick and intense because my host was being chased through the forest by a band of five or six men on horseback. The men were armed with bows, spears, and swords. They were dressed in leather and cloth clothing of a much finer quality than my host's, and over their clothes they wore chainmail vests and various pieces of light armor. Their heads were encased in simple metal helmets. The horsemen's clothes and armor gave me a sense, at last, of the period of time in which my host lived—medieval Europe—and their raucous shouts contained words I recognized as antiquated English, though I could not easily follow them.

Their meaning was perfectly clear, however, from the pure panic that filled my host as he fled before the horsemen. At the same time, under the panic, there was the sense that the horsemen represented pain and humiliation rather than injury or mortal danger. This was a scene that had played out many times in the past. The horsemen were soldiers employed by the local lord, or perhaps a king, to guard the lord's forest from poachers, and my host, who lived in the forest, had frequent run-ins with them over the years. The guards recognized my host as a peasant hermit and knew he wasn't a poacher, at least of the bigger game, so they tolerated his presence. But every time they spotted him, they would run him down and have a bit of bullying fun with him before they let him go.

My host kept looking back over his shoulder at the horsemen chasing him, who wore expressions of tormentor's glee. Sure enough, the horses easily overtook my host, and the men caught him. He struggled only weakly as they tied a rope around his wrists because he knew resistance was futile and would only earn him more pain. Then they tossed the rope over a branch, hoisted my host off the ground, and began to ride around his dangling body, laughing, jeering, and shouting and beating him with their bows and the shafts of their spears.

The beating was not especially severe in a physical sense, and luckily, I was somewhat shielded from the pain, which came through to me as dull impacts. It was intended to hurt and humiliate rather than harm, and it did its work well. My host was filled with shame that he'd allowed the men to see him at all in the first place, that they'd caught him, and that he once again had to suffer their bullying and taunts.

At last, ten or fifteen minutes later, they released him and rode away laughing, leaving him humiliated and lying on the leaves and grass. That's when I departed, came back to my own body, and woke.

There is really only one question to ask about such an experience: Was it an actual glimpse into a life I lived in the past? It was certainly vivid and richly filled with detail that was gritty, realistic, and non-anachronistic. My host felt very real and much like I do to myself, though simpler, illiterate, unworldly, and without a sense of history.

On the other hand, the experience contained no detail that I was not already aware of, since I have read extensively about medieval England. Robin Hood was a favorite historical character of my boyhood, and the experience was exactly like a forest peasant from Robin Hood's day being rousted by the Sheriff of Nottingham's men. And the fact that my host was simpler than I also could point to fantasy, for it would be difficult to imagine being inside a personality more complex than one's own. Perhaps that's why there are past life regressions but not future life progressions. My host's modest hovel even resembled the many forts I'd built in the woods when I was young, some of which were partially embedded in the ground.

However, I have to wonder if my love, in my current lifetime, of Robin Hood and building forts in the woods might not stem from unconscious memories of experiences in that past lifetime, if indeed it was real. And throughout my life, I've had other experiences, associations, and likes and dislikes that dovetail perfectly with the personality and life of the medieval peasant. One of the most interesting was a favorite and often-read book when I was in grade school: *My Side of the Mountain*, by Jean Craighead George. This book tells the story of a city boy who runs away to the Catskill Mountain wilderness, where he lives in a huge, hollowed-out tree. He even keeps a pet falcon in a wicker cage. Did I imagine my past life with those details because of the book, or did I love the book because it subconsciously reminded me of that past life?

In addition, I have an instinctive and unusually strong dislike of police authority and aristocratic prerogatives. In fact, when I was in high school and college, I was regularly harassed by the police for being different—a hippie. Seven Los Angeles cops harassed a buddy and me for half an hour one night, and in Houston, a police officer stopped me for jaywalking across an intersection that did not have a pedestrian walk light. He threatened to arrest me for possession of drugs—whether I had any drugs on me or not—and beat me within an inch of my life because he didn't like the way I looked or acted. I suppose he was just having some cruel fun with me, because after terrorizing me for fifteen or twenty minutes, he finally let me go. And more than once I've been chased through the night by armed rednecks intent on doing me harm. Maybe some of these people were reincarnations of those men on horseback who strung me up and beat me with their weapons. Or their ilk, who seem all to predominant these days.

And last, not only do I basically resemble the peasant in my general appearance and my love of solitude, my sewing is just as bad as his.

In the final analysis, I can't say if the experience was genuine or not. But while many dreams and waking fantasies have come and gone, the scenes I "saw" during that past-life regression have since remained a vivid part of my memory, and they feel more like real recollections than they do fantasies.

The Old Hag

THE FOLLOWING EVENT OCCURRED ON an ordinary weekday night in the early 1980s, when Julie and I lived in a bungalow on Jennings Street, in southeast Houston. I'd gone to bed around nine pm since I tended to get up before dawn. Julie joined me some time later, though I don't know when—probably after I'd been asleep for a couple of hours. I was barely disturbed by her getting into bed, and I continued to sleep for another few hours until just before two am, when I woke in sudden fear.

I was lying on my back, my body leaden from waking from a deep sleep. My mouth was open, and I felt as if something was clogging my throat. My nostrils were choked with a strong, cloyingly sweet odor through which I could barely breathe. I opened my eyes. The room was dimly lit by light filtering in from outside—a combination of moonbeams and the outdoor light on our garage. I couldn't see clearly, but I could discern the room's basic features.

I instantly was aware of a dark, amorphous shape hovering over my chest and face. The shape was not transparent, but it wasn't like a solid object, either. It was as if a patch of dense, willful shadow had become semi-tangible, independent, and motile.

It reminded me of a buzzard in size and basic shape, and it even had winglike appendages jutting from the backs of its shoulders that draped the sides of my head. These wings were not feathered like wings of a bird. Instead, they seemed like tattered black rags that had a rustling, fluttering, caressing life of their own. The body of this shape crouched on my chest, and I could even feel its weight, though it wasn't great. I also felt pressure on my shoulders—not like I was being pinned to the mattress, but as if I were being held still—or gripped, as a mosquito grips its prey.

A glaring intensity projected from where the thing's eyes ought to be, though I could not see actual eyes. Its facial features were blanked out by this glaring intensity, but below that, I could see a shaft like a huge proboscis, thrust down my throat. I felt as if the thing was sucking the breath—or perhaps, life—out of me. I had a definite impression of "femaleness" as well as of malevolence emanating from it.

With a force of will, I shut my mouth, and as I did, the shaft swiftly withdrew from my throat. I swept my arm across my chest, and the thing pressed harder against me for a split second, then launched itself away from me, just like a bird taking off. With a rustling flutter, it flew into a dark corner, where it vanished almost instantly by blending into the shadows. The cloying odor wafted away, and once again I could breathe clearly.

By now, I was fully awake. Julie still slept, undisturbed, next to me. I could not fall asleep again for some time, afraid that whatever had perched on me might come back. Eventually, I did sleep, this time on my stomach. At the time, I had no idea what had occurred, but I eventually learned that I had been visited by the Old Hag.

Modern psychology attributes the sensations of the Old Hag to sleep paralysis. This, and most of the subsequent information on sleep paralysis, is from *Wikipedia*'s entry:

> Sleep paralysis is a phenomenon in which people, either when falling asleep or wakening, temporarily experience a sense of inability to move, similar to when an arm or leg goes to sleep, but not associated with numbness. More formally, it is a transition state between wakefulness and rest characterized by complete muscle atonia (muscle weakness). It can occur at sleep onset or when awakening. It is believed a result of disrupted REM sleep, which is normally characterized by complete muscle atonia that prevents individuals from acting out their dreams. Sleep paralysis has been linked to disorders such as narcolepsy, migraines, anxiety disorders, and obstructive sleep apnea; however, it can also occur in isolation.

Psychologists go to great lengths to define the pathophysiology of sleep paralysis, but the condition's cause remains unknown. It has, they contend, two classifications: isolated sleep paralysis (ISP) and recurrent isolated sleep paralysis (RISP). ISPs are of short duration, usually a minute or so, but can persist for up to half an hour. They might affect an individual only once in a lifetime. RISP, on the other hand, afflicts some people throughout their lives, has a duration of as long as an hour, and has a higher incidence of out-of-body experiences. RISPs, more than ISPs, are associated with intruder and incubus/succubus hallucinations, which are nearly ubiquitous.

Scientists studying sleep paralysis tend to chalk up the hallucinations to hypnogogic and hypnopompic mental states, and some propose that the hallucinations might be an explanation for perceptions of ghosts and alien abductions, despite the fundamental reported differences among these various phenomena. The fear, they say, is brought on by the sense that an intruder of some sort is present while the subject is paralyzed—although some eye movement is possible during the episodes, the subject is incapable of moving or speaking. Scientists assert that the incubus/succubus hallucination occurs because the muscles that control breathing are partially paralyzed, leading to a belief that something is trying to suffocate them.

The Old Hag has been prevalent in the folklore of almost every culture, from the Americas to Europe, Asia, Africa, the Middle East, and East Asia. In almost every instance, the Old Hag is perceived as being female, be it termed a witch, a ghost, a succubus, or a minor demon. The condition is obviously fairly prevalent, which would certainly be the case if it is, as some scientists believe, an inappropriate overlap between the REM and waking stages of sleep, which could be expected to affect a certain proportion of any given population. But again, they are not sure what causes it.

An alternate explanation that I believe may be more accurate and arguably more profound is that there *are* entities in this reality that are not corporeal, in the common sense of the term, and that interact with humans in ways not yet perceived, much less understood. We are surrounded by a constant flux of energy inhabited on many levels by many sorts of beings, not all of whom are benevolent. Many, in fact, might prey on humans in one way or another—perhaps, like a psychic vampire, sucking life from its victim, or perhaps, like a parasite, consuming human vitality in other ways. Isn't addiction an example of the spirit being consumed to feed a non-corporeal something other than the self?

Think also about sudden unexpected death syndrome (SUNDS), which affects adults and adolescents as well as infants. SUNDS produces a particularly high mortality rate among young men from East Asia—especially those from Thailand, Laos, and the Philippines. Scientists believe that SUNDS is generated by natural causes, although no associations have been found with organic heart disease or structural heart problems. It is, however, almost universally attributed by the folk cultures in these countries to the Old Hag.

I have not studied the condition in depth. I have only my one personal experience and a little reading to go by, but I can say that I was awake and aware and that I'm convinced I perceived a non-corporeal creature squatting on my chest and sucking out my breath —or vitality. I can't prove it was really there, but it sure seemed like it. I could feel its weight, and I could see it. When I moved to push it away, it took off and fled into the shadows, just as a mosquito would had I swatted at it while it sucked my blood.

In the end, the Old Hag seems to me to be as valid an explanation as the scientific one for these nocturnal visitations, especially since the researchers can't really explain the basis for their proposals. Perhaps some instances of sleep paralysis are produced by medical or other tangible conditions, but that does not negate the possibility that there are nasty, seldom-seen creatures that can take advantage of the unconsciousness of human sleep, just as a mosquito tends to land on a part of the body not readily visible to the victim—and for a very similar reason: to sneakily creep up, alight, and suck out some part of one's life. And just like mosquitoes, the Old Hag flits through the shadows until they find an opportunity to prey on their unsuspecting victims.

Do they come from the shadows, or do they somehow have access to our plane of existence from some netherworld or from another, very different reality? Is it possible that there are creatures that have lives that intersect more than one plane of reality? Perhaps science just hasn't realized that such creatures and beings are as real as we are even if they do not seem overtly tangible to us. We'd better take notice, though, because some, apparently, can greatly affect us and our reality through means too subtle to easily perceive.

Haunted: No. 10

I CHUCKLED AS I APPROACHED the steps leading to
the second level of the small brick apartment complex
in Houston. It was like deja vu, only this was neither
false memory nor any sort of precognition. This was
real. Evening had fallen, but the air of early fall was
still heavy with heat and humidity. I didn't need to
check the number on the door as I rang the bell for
No. 10, a big grin on my face. I hoped Charles was
home. What a surprise he was going to get!

Charles and I had shared experiences and late-
night philosophy for a couple of years until circumstances separated us. Now, a year later, in spring 1974,
I had run into a mutual friend who knew where
Charles was living. When this friend told me the address, I was taken aback—it was an apartment I had
lived in briefly almost three years earlier, just prior to
meeting Charles.

So here I was, visiting a familiar friend in a familiar
habitat, though the two had remained unconnected
until now. The door opened, and there Charles stood.

His eyes lit up as he recognized me, and he ushered me into the apartment.

We brought each other up to date and discussed the fact that his present roommate was moving out the following week, leaving the second bedroom vacant. He asked if I was interested in moving in. Although I only recently had moved into the apartment I currently occupied, the prospect of sharing rooms with Charles more than offset my reluctance to pack up my belongings once more and trundle them across town. But something else made me hesitate.

I'd lived in this apartment before with my former girlfriend, Linda, toward the end of my relationship with her. After Linda and I moved in, we found swastikas and pentagrams roughly gouged into the wood of the insides of the bedroom and closet doors.

I'd stayed in the apartment only about two months, and I didn't really remember much about living there. It was the first time I had lived in an intimate relationship with someone, and Linda and I often were at odds with each other during our cohabitation. In fact, the only vivid memory I had of the place was of an incident that had taken place while I was writing a term paper for one of my university classes. I found myself waking, as if from a daze, standing in the hallway and clutching a sheaf of papers in my left hand and a pen in my right. It was almost as if I had awakened from sleepwalking, except that I had started out fully conscious in the bedroom that served as my study, writing the paper instead of sleeping.

I remember how strange it felt to find myself standing there and realizing that I had been wandering around the apartment for several hours in a benumbed, almost fugue state, scribbling my paper all the while. Instead of the required ten-page report on a literary work, I had written a thirty-page opus of social and spiritual protest.

My main recollections of the apartment were unsettling, but I chalked them up to my frequent depression and failing relationship with Linda, so I agreed to move in as soon as Charles's current roommate moved out. In the meantime, he and I reestablished our friendship. A few days after our reunion, I visited Charles at the apartment. We sat in the living room for a couple of hours, talking nonstop. At last, I got up to go to the bathroom. The layout of the apartment was simple enough. The back half consisted of two bedrooms flanking a central bathroom, with a short hall connecting all three. The front half was the combination living–dining room and the kitchen, which opened to the left, off the dining area. It was an average but nice-looking and bright apartment, one of ten in a small complex that had been built in the modernist style in the late 1950s or early 1960s.

I came out of the bathroom, walked into the living room, and sat down. Charles wasn't in the room, but from where I sat, I could see a slice of the bedroom where his roommate slept—the same one that had been my study when I'd live there with Linda. Someone was moving around in it, and since the roommate wasn't home, I assumed it was Charles, though I thought it odd because that wasn't his room. But I shrugged it away and resumed our conversation where I'd left off. Rather than raise my voice to yell into the other room, I got up and walked into the hallway to be able to talk more easily. As I entered the hall, I stopped dead in my tracks, my sentence choked off. I could see the whole room, and no one was in it!

With my mind doing a double-take, I stepped back into the living room. As I did, Charles came out of the kitchen. Seeing the shocked look on my face, he asked what was the matter.

I told him I'd seen, or thought I had, someone in his roommate's room. No, it was definite. The more I thought about it, the more certain I was that someone had been in that room. It had been more than a momentary flash. I'd looked directly at the figure for at least ten seconds, although it was partially obscured by the doorjamb. When Charles asked me to describe what I had seen, I didn't hesitate since Charles wasn't one to scoff at the unknown.

It's strange how the mind can record an image even if the attention isn't fully focused on it at the time. When I'd seen the figure in the bedroom, my attention had been on my conversation. Seeing movement in the room, I had naturally assumed it was Charles and really didn't pay attention until I found the room empty. But as I dug into my memory of the image, I wondered how I could have been so blind.

Charles was chunky and of average height for a male, but the figure I'd seen was slender and only about four feet tall. Visually, it was much like a three-dimensional shadow, dark at the center and lightening to a gray at the edges. It was humanoid in proportions, although no limbs were distinctly apparent. I realized also that I had gotten a few impressions that were not visual but on a "feeling" level. The first was of long, straight, dark hair falling over the shoulders; the second was that it was a woman; and the third was that she was lost and lonely.

I asked Charles if he had noticed anything unusual in the apartment, and he said that visitors had heard sounds and seen what seemed like the same apparition. I told him about what had happened to me when I'd lived there with Linda. We then examined the closet doors. Most of them must have been replaced, since they were free of marks. But on the inside of the one in Charles's bedroom—the room Linda and I had slept in—a swastika remained.

In the rush of moving the following week, I forgot the incident. Within two weeks, I was fairly settled in, and life went smoothly as the fall semester progressed. I kept busy with school work and my job as a grading assistant for an English professor, so when other odd things began happening, they barely registered at first.

One morning when I got up, the front door was standing wide open. I was immediately miffed at Charles, who had come home after I'd gone to bed, and I spoke to him about the dangers of burglary and such. I'd been robbed before, and I didn't want it to happen again. He said he thought he'd closed and locked the door when he got home, but I thought it more likely that he'd shut the door, but not completely, and the wind had blown it open during the night.

But then, with increasing frequency over the next two or three months, we woke to discover the door wide open. Many nights, I would check the door the last thing before going to bed to make certain it was securely shut and locked. Even so, often it would be wide open in the morning, as many as three times a week.

About the time we realized there was definitely something odd about our front door, we began to hear noises around the apartment. The noises were mostly knocks or sounds of things falling. The sounds were neither loud nor violent but were forceful enough to draw attention. They also invariable took place in a room that was unoccupied at the time, although usually they came from the living room. Never did we find a fallen object that might account for the sound. Nor did the sounds come from adjacent apartments. No. 10 was on the second floor at the end of the building, and the apartment was not flanked by another apartment except beside the kitchen.

Then, one night after I'd lived in the apartment for about six weeks, I was lying in bed reading, and something more sinister happened. My room was the one in which I and others had seen the apparition, though I usually didn't think much about that. But this night, I felt a presence enter the room, stand at the foot of my bed, and look down at me. I thought then about the apparition, but this thing now watching me didn't "feel" the same. This felt masculine and watchful, not feminine and lost.

I stared directly at, or through, it but could see nothing. The feeling persisted for several minutes and then was gone. I returned to my book, but not without vague sensations of paranoia.

I didn't mention the presence to Charles, but we did talk more and more about the door being open, the noises, and our growing feelings of uneasiness in the apartment. We began spending less and less time there, and soon the place got to be a shambles, with our possession strewn all over the place.

During the next two months, I was visited many times by the masculine presence, which would come into the room, often while I was reading before bedtime, stand at the foot of the bed, and watch me. Initially, I often spoke to it, telling it I knew it was there and asking what it wanted. Later, though, it gave me such uneasy feelings that I would just order it out. Usually it would go when I told it to.

One day, my friend, Ralph, came over for a visit. Ralph, a pragmatic individual, had a strong sense of concrete reality and no belief in the supernatural. At the time, he was a graduate student in sociology at the University of Houston. I'd never mentioned anything to him about the strange activities going on in the apartment.

We were talking when, suddenly, he stared toward my bedroom and partly rose out of his chair, nervously saying he'd seen someone in my bedroom. I knew there was no one else in the apartment.

From Ralph's description, I gathered he'd seen the feminine apparition that I and other people had observed: about four feet tall, darkly shrouded, with no real features, standing at about the same place in the room where I'd seen it. I now knew I hadn't been imagining it, but that didn't make me feel any better because I had to sleep in that room. And the masculine presence was entering with greater frequency.

One night about a month after Ralph saw the apparition, Charles and I went to our rooms to go to bed at around the same time. I lay reading for some minutes before I became aware that the masculine presence had entered my room and was staring down at me. I lay my book face down on my chest and stared directly at the space it seemed to occupy. Rather harshly, because I was annoyed and disturbed by these invasions of my privacy, I demanded to know what it wanted.

Suddenly I felt transfixed and paralyzed. A bar of vibrating coldness lanced diagonally through my brain, from the left hinge of my jaw to the upper right corner of my forehead. The vibrating bar seemed to be the same diameter and length as an unused pencil, and it felt gray and frigid as it buzzed inside my head.

As this happened, I became aware of two things. The first was a distant babble of multitudinous voices. I hesitate to use the word demonic—no words or ideas were clear, and the babble didn't seem overtly evil, though there was an insanely confused quality to its subdued pandemonium. The second sensation was of a presence inside my brain. With a shock, I realized it was holding me motionless, attempting to control me.

Terrified, I struggled to regain a grip on my mind and body. But even as the thing inside tried to pry me loose from my own moorings, I remembered a passage from a book on astral travel I'd read a few years earlier. In this passage, the author dispelled the fear that a disembodied spirit could take over a body whose spirit was traveling astrally. The author stated that a person's body was his own and couldn't be taken over unless he was willing to have such a thing happen.

I wasn't. With this passage in mind, I firmly pressed my consciousness into its own seat and refused to budge. All the while, I brought pressure to bear on the thing inside my head, forcing it out of me, mentally declaring over and over, "This is my mind! Get out! Get out!"

Gradually the intrusive presence slackened and faded entirely, and I could move again. The buzzing, cold bar of sensation continued for a number of minutes longer, then it too waned, leaving a residual feeling that persisted for some minutes afterward.

I checked the clock. About thirty or forty minutes had elapsed since I lay down to read, which meant that the attack had lasted for about fifteen minutes. I was shaken and afraid to sleep. Then I heard a couple of muffled, indistinct words spoken by a voice somewhere else in the apartment. My bedroom door was closed, so I couldn't tell where the voice came from or whose it had been.

Afraid to get up and look but more afraid not to know, I rose and opened the bedroom door. Down the short hall, Charles's door was shut, and all was quiet. I went into the living room, half expecting the front door to be open, but it was shut and locked.

Then I went to check on Charles. I'd heard words, and he was the only other person in the apartment. Not wanting to wake him if he was asleep, I knocked softly on his door and quietly called his name. When he didn't respond, I knocked again and tried the knob.

His door was unlocked, and as I opened it, light from the hall fanned across the room. He was lying in a half fetal position on the bed, oddly with his head at the foot. His face was turned away and in shadow, so I couldn't see it. I spoke his name several times, but he didn't move. Rationalizing that he was all right and just sleeping, I shut the door and returned to my room. I was still uneasy, but for some reason, I didn't feel as if the thing was going to come back—at least that night. Finally, exhaustion overtook me, and I slept.

Charles was gone when I rose the next morning, and I didn't see him until the afternoon. Shortly after I arrived home from classes, he came home from work, and before I could say a word, he asked if I'd noticed anything unusual the night before. Instead of telling him what I'd experienced, I asked him what he meant.

He told me that just as he was on the verge of sleep, he had been attacked by an entity that had tried to take over his mind. He'd heard an incessant babble of voices, experienced paralysis, and battled a presence that tried to gain control over his body. He'd cried out, trying to attract my attention, and was dimly aware of my entering his room a few minutes later to check on him, but he'd been unable to move or speak to let me know he needed help. He thought it had taken him about an hour to fight off the entity.

I related my experience, and together, we pieced together what might have happened. A spirit or entity of some sort had first attacked me. Because I was fully conscious, I'd been able to fight it off. Then it turned on Charles, who, being almost asleep, was more vulnerable. Consequently, he'd had a more difficult time defending himself.

We agreed that the entity, while malevolent, had not been powerful enough to be really evil in the full sense of the word. It actually seemed weak, since I'd fought it off with relative ease, and it managed to get a grip on Charles only because he wasn't fully conscious. We wondered if the attack was related to the feminine apparition, the masculine presence, the open front door, or the noises, but we could come to no firm conclusions.

But that didn't mean we wanted to live in the same apartment with evil entities, no matter how weak, so we decided to move. Within two weeks, we were gone, but the apartment was not through with us quite yet. Oddly, for several more years, we met people who'd lived in that same apartment, and although none had specific stories to tell, all had felt uneasy there, and none lived in it longer than two or three months. In fact, during a four-year period, the apartment had more than ten sets of tenants. Charles and I lived there about five months.

The day we moved, my girlfriend came over to help. She arrived before I did, and when I got there, she was sitting on the steps, and the door to the apartment was wide open. She said she found it that way. At first, she'd gone inside, but she soon came back out because the place made her feel creepy.
I wasn't surprised.

Charles' account:

I can't add a different narrative to what Chris has written. It is as I remember it. I would just add that many people who came over saw the shadow in the back. It happened before he moved in, but I discounted it at the time. When my previous roommate and I lived there, that was the main thing that happened, but I remember my roommate's sister staying with us and commenting that there were noises, like things falling, footsteps, and bumps.

On this particular night, I had lain down, and was practicing meditation techniques before going to sleep. My eyes were closed, and I was lying still, trying to watch my mind wander. I drifted into a semiconscious state, and before long, I heard a buzzing sound. I knew it was coming from inside my head. I then lost consciousness. I was no longer tracking events, but neither was I asleep. I was physically paralyzed, heard a babble of voices, and felt a presence. I had been practicing controlling my consciousness in these states, but this time I had no control.

I tried to wake up but could not. I tried to move but could not. I continued to resist for the longest time. I tried to call out for Chris, whom I knew was in the next room, but could not. Chris came into my room, but I could not respond. Gradually, many minutes later it seemed, my fight for control pushed the buzzing sound away, and I was able to sit up, awake. I felt the thing that was controlling me move out of my head and out of my room before I sat up.

I might be able to attribute the front door being open so much to the building settling, but it happened too often. Each time this happened, we would check the door, and it would fit the lock when we closed and tested it. As for the entity, I believe that it was weak; its only hold on me was that I was already in a dream state and susceptible to suggestion, as with hypnosis.

It has always bothered me that such a new apartment would have something like that. There had been an older neighborhood there, and at first, I attributed the apartment's weirdness to a previous building. But a 1944 map shows it was a vacant lot at the time. This

means that the apartment building was the first structure on the lot.

Postscript

In 2004—thirty years after the incidents described
above—I mentioned to a friend that I'd lived in a
haunted apartment and described where it was. Her
eyes lit. She said she had friends in that same neighborhood who told her it was common knowledge
among residents of the neighborhood that a certain
apartment there was haunted. She didn't know which
one, and unfortunately, I didn't have the time to inves-
tigate further. But I bet I know which one it is.

The Spirit of Bruja Canyon

WEST TEXAS IS A LAND of huge spaces and big sky, of gunfighters, mystery, and adventure. Billy the Kid spent his only night in jail in a West Texas town, and countless other bandits roamed the region searching for new crimes to commit or fleeing across the Rio Grande to the legal anonymity, if not exactly safety, of Mexico. It was the stamping ground of the legendary Pecos Bill and the notorious Judge Roy Bean and remains the center of legends of buried gold and lost mines. And no part of West Texas is as spectacular, or as mysterious, as Big Bend.

Named in 1849 by Lt. William Whiting, Big Bend is the area of Texas bounded on the south by the large bend in the Rio Grande as it runs southeast from El Paso, then northeast to Del Rio. Its northern border extends from El Paso, through Candelaria, Alpine, and Sanderson, then on to Del Rio. In the 1930s, the tip of Big Bend, comprising three-quarters of a million acres, was turned into a national park.

But despite the existence of the park service and a few paved roads, the area is as rugged and foreboding as it was when it was first surveyed in 1899. There are hot springs along the river, and the entire western side of the park is the product of volcanism, evident in the jut of rock, domes of hardened volcanic mud and ash, blackened iron-bearing rock strewn over the ground, and miles of geological dikes scarifying the landscape.

My friend, Charles, and I loved Big Bend and had made several trips to the park. The rugged terrain and recent wild history appealed to our sense of adventure. On our earliest trips, we'd concentrated on the eastern side of the park and the Chisos Mountains, which lie roughly in the center of the park. On one of those visits, however, we had stayed briefly on the western side of the park, near the mouth of Santa Elena Canyon, where Terlingua Creek empties into the Rio Grande. We'd even hiked several miles up the creek to visit the ghost town of Terlingua Abajo, which had been the center of a small floodplain farming community that clustered on both sides of the creek.

In spring 1978, we decided to more fully explore the western side of the park. In particular, we wanted to get on top of Mesa de Anguilla, through which the Rio Grande cuts Santa Elena Canyon. Then we intended to hike back along the mesa to the river and look down on it from the canyon rim. Studying a U.S. Geological Survey map, we found a possible access to the mesa top: a steep cut that sliced up the mesa wall a short day's hike west of Terlingua Abajo.

We left our car at Terlingua Abajo early in the morning, shouldered our packs, and set out. As we moved through the barren ruins of this small town, we reflected on how strange it seemed that this had actually been a farming community. Even as late as the 1920s, the land was arable. But the miners who came to this region to dig cinnabar from the ground and melt the mercury from it had cut almost all the trees from the slopes of the Chisos for their mining operations, and poor techniques by the farmers who fed them rapidly depleted the floodplain soil.

All the buildings of Terlingua Abajo save one are adobe and are now mostly fallen and crumbled. The one exception is the tiny church, which was constructed of rock, although it too was half collapsed at the time. Right next to the church was a small cemetery consisting of about twenty graves. Only the dead inhabit Terlingua Abajo now.

As we passed the church, we took a line-of-sight bearing on the cut we sought. It was visible in the distance as a black scar running up the sheer mesa wall. Walking was difficult at first. We were carrying enough supplies and water for four days—one day out, two on the mesa, and one day back—and that much water is heavy. But after a couple of miles, we were well into the swing of things, and the packs rode more easily on our backs as the desert world opened before us.

Initially, the terrain consisted of dusty flats dotted every few hundred yards with mounded hills a hundred feet or more high. Although we had to climb an occasional low ridge, things went smoothly for several hours. Shortly after midday, we had a tense encounter after a baby javelina scurried across our path about forty feet in front of us. Its mama was right on its heels, and she stopped, snorted threateningly, and pawed a cloud of dust into the air with her sharp hooves. Just when we were sure she was going to charge, her baby disappeared into the scrub brush and cactus, and a few moments later, she followed.

As we neared the cut, the terrain flattened considerably, although the ground now was crisscrossed by a network of four- to eight-foot-deep gullies that were difficult to negotiate. When we finally reached the cut, we found that the gullies carried runoff rainwater from the mesa to now-distant Terlingua Creek, but while we were scrambling in and out of them in the desert heat, their purpose seemed to be to give us trouble. Gradually, they shallowed as we neared the foot of the mesa.

At last, we arrived at the bottom of the talus slope below the cut, where water had gouged a large crescent out of the base of the slope on the right side and smoothed part of the rocky desert floor with a bed of fine sand. Extending up the talus slope to the base of the cut itself was a lengthy fall of boulders looking almost as if a large cataract had lumpily solidified. This fall of boulders ran upward almost half a mile before it stopped at the bottom of the dark gash. The sum of the parts formed the head of a small but picturesque canyon.

We rested before we attempted to scramble over the fall of boulders, assay the cut, and climb to the top of the mesa. From the bottom, it looked as if it would take half an hour to haul our packs over the boulders to the base of the cut, and we'd have to go at least that far before we could judge whether or not we could climb up the cut itself.

After the rest, we began our scramble. The rocks at the bottom were relatively small, from pebble-size to several feet in diameter, but as we proceeded, the rocks were larger and larger, eventually becoming boulders of immense size. By the time we reached the top of the talus slope, the boulders were from eight to twenty feet and so tossed and jumbled that they created cave-like passages. As we went, crouching, the last hundred feet through these passages, we heard a strange droning sound that increased in volume. At last, we stood at the actual base of the cut and could look up it.

A trickle of runoff water seeped down the cut to pool briefly before soaking into the sandy earth at the top of the talus slope. At the edges of the tiny pool, literally hundreds of bees and wasps drank and daubed the mud to make their dwellings along the cliff walls. Thousands more hovered above the pool and in the air in front of their cliff dwellings. These insects were the source of the droning we'd heard. We were standing in a veritable cloud of them; yet strangely, they seemed completely peaceful and nonaggressive.

We slowly took off our packs and leaned them against a boulder, then we peered up the cut to see if we could climb it. We could see up it only about sixty feet before it took a turn. Noting that the wasps, for some reason, weren't in the crevasse itself, I decided to step across the pool, climb up to the bend, and survey the cut further.

I lifted my foot to step across the water, and instantly the peaceful drone of the wasps colored with anger. A number of them flew menacingly at me, although none of them tried to sting me. I lowered my foot and stepped back, and the wasps instantly grew peaceful. I tried to step forward again, and again they became angry, flying at my face, keeping me away. As soon as I stepped back, peaceful drones replaced the angry sounds, and all was well.

There seemed to be nothing we could do. We both tried several more times to climb into the cut, but the wasps just wouldn't let us pass. I guess the strange thing was that, despite their sheer numbers and the fact that we angered them much of the hour we spent in their company, the wasps never stung either of us.

At last, frustrated in our attempt to climb the cut, we started back down the fall of boulders, skirting a rattlesnake that lay sunning in our path about halfway down. Finally, we reached the crescent gouged out of the talus slope at the bottom of the canyon.

By this time, the sun had disappeared behind the mesa. We were tired, so we set up camp. We finished our meal about dusk and lay down on our sleeping bags to relax and chat. With the water gouge at our backs, comfortable temperatures, and a patch of soft sand under us, we were quite comfortable.

As night fell, a nearly full moon rose, illuminating the mesa wall and desert floor clearly in its light. Sometime between 8:00 and 8:30, I glimpsed a movement out of the corner of my left eye. I had been lying on my right side, propped up on my elbow, facing Charles. He was lying on his sleeping bag, talking about legendary holy men from the Far East.

When I saw the movement over my left shoulder, I thought it was a tall stalk of grass right next to me, waving in the slight breeze. I turned to look but saw nothing of the sort. I turned back to Charles, and we continued our conversation, but out of the corner of my eye I could still see something moving slightly.

I looked again but saw only the familiar, moonlit desert. About the only thing I noticed in the right direction was a creosote bush about fifty feet away. Still, when my attention was directed at Charles, something kept moving in the corner of my vision. I even got up a couple of times and walked toward the bush. I never actually approached the bush to examine it before I'd go back to my sleeping bag. It seemed like just another scrubby creosote that was way too sparse to conceal even a small child.

Back on my sleeping bag, I tried turning my head slowly, watching straight ahead but paying attention to what my peripheral vision brought to me. Maybe I could sort of sneak up on whatever was puzzling my sight. As my head turned, I was astounded to see a man standing where I had seen the scrubby-looking bush! I stared sharply in that direction, but now only the bush was visible.

Thinking I had been imagining the man, I looked back at Charles, who was still talking about holy men. There was that movement again! I turned slowly and could see in my peripheral vision the man standing where the bush had been. For several minutes, I experimented, discovering that if I looked directly at the man, he appeared to be the bush, but if I used my peripheral vision, I could make him out quite clearly.

He looked to be in his sixties and was fairly short and slightly stocky. He could have been Mexican or Indian. He was dressed like a Mexican peasant, in light-colored pants, a loose tan shirt, and a serape. A sombrero hung over his back. His face was grizzled, his hair was white, and his eyes were like black voids.

I realized I also could sense his presence. For some reason, I wasn't alarmed, although I thought he'd be scary to approach. At one point, I considered getting up and going over to him, now that I knew he was there, but something told me he wouldn't be there when I arrived. He radiated a great power that was frightening, but I also sensed that he wasn't inclined to direct that power against us, which was reassuring.

I continued to observe the watcher as best as I could, marveling at the discrepancy between direct and peripheral vision and seeing him in turn as a man and a bush. Then, about half an hour to forty minutes after I'd first noticed movement, I realized the man was gone. At first, I felt his absence; then, looking, I no longer saw him or the bush.

During the whole episode, I said nothing to Charles about the man, at first because I didn't want to address the subject in the man's presence, then later because I didn't want Charles to think I was spooked over nothing. Half an hour later, we turned in for the night.

In the morning, we struck camp. The night before, we had discussed hiking farther down the mesa wall to try to find another way to the top, but the map showed that there wasn't another access point close by, so without talking about it, we returned to the car at Terlingua Abajo. On the way back to the car, Charles asked if I had seen someone the day before.

I said no, not during the day, but during the night, I'd seen someone watching us. He replied that he, too, had seen a man watching our camp, but that he couldn't see the fellow directly, only out of the edges of his sight. I asked for a description, and Charles's matched mine almost exactly, even to the sensation of dangerous but non-malevolent power coming from the man. He'd also seen the man for a little over half an hour, but in addition, he had spotted him several times as we approached the canyon. These sighting had been in the form of passing glimpses, but when Charles did double takes to look again, he couldn't see anyone, only plants.

We discussed the possibility of returning to the area but decided to spend the night at a campground to ready our gear and clean up. The following day we would return. It would be the night of the full moon.

The next morning, we got into the car to drive back to Terlingua Abajo, and I turned the key in the ignition, but nothing happened. I tried again, and still nothing, not even a click. The car wouldn't start, although it had given no sign of problems until now. In fact, I'd tuned it up prior to our trip to the park.

Feeling as if we were being told not to return to the canyon, we got a jump start and left the park. During the thirteen-hour drive back to Houston, we stopped only for gas. After we left the park, the car started without trouble. It may have been my imagination, but the entire way home, I felt as if we were being pursued.

Two years later, Charles and I returned to the canyon with a friend, Mike. We didn't see anything unusual this time, but we did discover the name of the canyon. A ranger said it was called Bruja Canyon. Bruja is Spanish for witch.

A final weird note was that, of the many photographs I took of the area during our two visits—nearly three rolls of film were used to photograph the canyon and its approach—not a single one came out, although other pictures on two of the rolls developed just fine.

Charles's account of the incident:

Chris and I loved exploring Big Bend National Park. I had acquired topographic maps of the park and noticed an interesting place on the west side. There was a large fault scarp that had been dissected by the Rio Grande. This meant that there was a huge mesa surrounded by the river and the fault scarp. I saw only one possible hiking trail up from the park side, and that was to climb up through an unnamed cleft, where a stream would pour off the top of the mesa.

We planned a trip and went to Big Bend. We parked the car at Terlingua Abajo, a small floodplain farming village that was tied to Terlingua, an early twentieth-century mining town farther north along Terlingua Creek. It was a long, slow hike across the hot, flat desert because there were many small arroyos. It seemed as if we were going up and down as much as we were moving forward. The fault scarp rises some 1,500 feet straight up, and from far away, we could see the notch that was our destination.

We went directly to the fault scarp and walked along its talus slope to the notch. At one point, I got far ahead of Chris, and I began to experience something I attributed to the heat. I kept seeing a figure, dressed like a 1900s Mexican peasant, out of the corner of my eye. I would turn my head to look, and it would only be a Spanish dagger or an ocotillo, the two forms of vegetation in Big Bend that get as tall as a man. This happened at least three times.

We eventually made it to the notch, and found it was a pour-off, with a trickle of water coming straight down hundreds of feet. More than that, there was a line of bees and wasps along the edge of the water, presumably drinking. I looked up and saw numerous rock ledges jutting a few inches out of the mesa wall, and they were lined with bee and wasp nests.

We considered using ropes to climb the notch—this was before rope climbing was popular—but we had never done that before. Other, more experienced, climbers have since found ways up, but there was another problem. Every time we approached the notch, the tone of the bees and wasps would get louder and more threatening. No way we could handle hundreds of bee and wasp stings. We gave up.

We settled into camp on a sandy island in the rock-strewn floor of the notch. The wall of the mesa was on both sides of us, since we were at the bottom of the notch. We set up our camp, lit our camp stove, and ate dinner, then lay on our pallets, talking about various things and watching the night.

I noticed that in the middle of our conversation, Chris would sometimes get up and walk away and then come back. I attributed this to his inquisitiveness about something he saw, but he didn't say what it was. At one point, I got up and was walking around, when I saw, out of the corner of my eye, the Mexican again. I was not hot and tired—I was rested—so I had the presence of mind not to look directly at him but to take in his details. He wore huaraches, a serape, white cotton pants, and a shirt. His face was a black hole, and the only details were his eyes, like two pinprick stars, as bright and piercing as any in the sky. When I looked directly at him, he was gone. This happened perhaps another three times during the night. I said nothing to Chris about it, but I knew this was something new. He seemed to be wondering who was invading his home. He seemed powerful but not threatening.

Nothing further happened that night. The next day, we packed up and headed back to the car. Halfway back, we stopped to rest, and I said to Chris, "We weren't alone last night." He said, yes, he knew. We then exchanged details on what we had seen. We described the man as wearing slightly different clothes, but the impression was the same. Chris said this was what he was investigating when he walked away from the camp several times.

A couple of years later, we returned. We stopped at the ranger station, and there were two rangers, one an Anglo National Park Service ranger, the other a local Mexican American employee who was emptying trash cans. We asked for a backcountry camping permit. The ranger asked where we wanted to camp, and I pointed to the notch in the mesa wall. "That's Bruja Canyon," the ranger exclaimed. The second ranger, who had been friendly up until then, hurriedly left the room. The first ranger said, "The local Mexicans call it that after a witch that used to live there. They will have nothing to do with it."

The second trip was uneventful compared with the first. This time we saw human and horse footprints on the way there and in the notch, which we now know as Bruja Canyon. We camped in the same spot, but nothing happened.

Looking back on it, I am convinced that what we experienced was an entity that was once a human being. It had will and was not simply an impression of a past resident. I believe that Chris and I felt the presence of this former resident, and our minds clothed him in early Mexican peasant clothes—for each of us, this was slightly different, and so our descriptions were similar but did not match perfectly. We both saw this entity out of the corners of our eyes. Yet we know that the brain manufactures both color and pattern, and peripheral vision is not what we actually see, but what our brain interpolates. Chris and my minds were trying to come to grips with an unexplainable presence, and thus draped it in the most familiar conventional imagery possible.

However, the mind could not interpolate away the entity's consciousness, its intelligence, the black hole of its face, or the piercing, starlike eyes that seemed for an instant like an endless universe. It was all over in half an hour, and I have never experienced anything like it before or after.

Postscript

In 2014, Charles emailed me to let me know that he and I had become a part, albeit minor, of Texas folklore. This tickled us both, since we both love Texas folklore.

It seems that a previous publication of this article has been quoted several times in books and Internet write-ups on Bruja Canyon. Here are several of them:

"The canyon has been thought haunted for hundreds of years. Bruja is Spanish for "witch," and the area can certainly be considered bewitched. Photographs taken here often cannot be developed, and unexplained flickering lights are observed. In 1978, two hikers encountered the silent apparition of a Mexican man wearing a serape and sombrero. Both witnesses sensed a 'dangerous but non-malevolent power' coming from the man."

—*Haunted Places: The National Directory—Ghostly Abodes, Sacred Sites, UFO Landings, and Other Supernatural Locations,* by Dennis William Hauck (Penguin Books, 1996). This passage is quoted verbatim in: "Bruja Canyon" (www.geocities.ws/Baja/Canyon/3741/area/texas/brujacanyon.html).

"Nearby lies Canyon de Brujas (Witch Canyon), often the site of moanful [sic] cries from an Apache maiden who is said to have drowned herself rather than be defiled by her white captors. The spirit of the maiden is said to wander the canyon in search of a way home to her Apache village.

—"Big Bend's Chisos Mountains: The Ghost Mountains of Far West Texas," by Logan Hawkee (www.wintertexasonline.com/bigbend.htm). (No longer an active site.)

"Big Bend National Park – Bruja Canyon: Bruja is Spanish for Witch. The area is thought to be bewitched. Photographs taken often cannot be developed. Unexplained flickering lights are seen. A sense of dangerous, non-malevolent power."

—"Texas Haunts," Arkansas Paranormal Investigations (www.paranormalbeliever.com/Texas-haunts.html).

"As recently as 1978, hikers reported seeing the apparition of a man wearing a serape in Bruja ("witch") Canyon. According to *Tales of Big Bend*, others have seen the daughter of a Spanish don who drowned herself in a pool rather than succumb to her bandit captors."

—"America's Scariest Trails: Big Bend's Deadly Past," by Anthony Cerretani (www.backpacker.com/november-09-big-bends-deadly-past/destinations/13377).

It turns out that even had Charles and I managed to get past the wasps at the pool, we probably couldn't have climbed far up the cleft. The upper portion of Brujo Canon is what is referred to as a "slot canyon," and it is a pretty rugged climb that requires traversing several deep pools and some rappelling. It is considered a Class 5 climb, which should be undertaken only by the truly experienced.

My Internet search also revealed that there are a number of recent photographs online of the canyon, which belies the notion that "photographs of the canyon can't be developed"—even though none of the many I took came out. However, all of the ones I saw online are of the upper canyon, not the lower section below the cliff, where Charles and I were. Also, I assume that most, if not all, of the recent photos were taken with digital cameras, not the old film camera that I'd carried. Perhaps that makes a difference.

Smiley

I CALL HIM SMILEY. MAYBE he's an it, but it looks like a he. He pays regular visits to our house, but it's not as if we've ever invited him. We'd been living in our house for something less than a year before I noticed him and a couple of other uninvited guests. Actually, maybe *we* were the uninvited guests.

The house on River Drive is fairly old, the original part built in about 1910. It has two stories and was one of the first houses in the area, which was incorporated as the small town of Park Place, Texas, a few years later and subsequently annexed by the city of Houston in 1934.

The original builder remains unknown to us—the signature on the oldest document in the hall of records is too faded with age to read. But the second owner—who added the second floor to the house—was Captain B, a pilot for ships plying the Houston Ship Channel, and the house was known for many years as the Captain's House. Indeed, the house is on Sims Bayou, one of the many shallow estuaries that drain into the Houston Ship Channel, which is just a couple of miles downstream. Captain B could have taken a boat to work had he wished.

In its heyday, the house was one of the better in the area. Several weddings took place there, including that of George Marquette, a prominent Houston city councilman of the mid 1900s. But a series of owners let the house fall into disrepair, and a fire that destroyed one of the upstairs rooms seemed to spell the end.

The house lay abandoned for nearly ten years until a local businesswoman purchased it for her mother to live in. The businesswoman performed basic repairs to the burned section of the house, but to no avail. Her mother didn't like the house and wouldn't stay there. The businesswoman then rented the house to a succession of tenants who were not kind to the old place, including a group of biker drug dealers who painted all the trim and hardwood floors black. Seeing potential in the property, Julie and I bought the house in 1994 and began the lengthy process of renovating it.

Our two daughters—Sydney and Mariko, then eleven and ten, respectively—occupied the two upstairs bedrooms, and Julie and I took one of the downstairs bedrooms. We used the second downstairs bedroom as our office. This second bedroom had a glass door to a side porch, but because we weren't using the door at the time and I needed more wall space, I fastened a sheet of plywood over it.

A few months after we moved in, a friend asked us who the old man with the beard was. She'd been driving by and seen him standing behind the living room window, watching the street. At the time, we had to say we didn't know, but we soon started noticing him ourselves.

Both my daughters and I occasionally felt his presence in the living room and caught faint whiffs of pipe smoke. Once Sydney actually saw his dim and transparent form. And a visiting friend, who knew nothing of the apparition, said he felt a strong presence of a bearded seafaring man smoking a pipe and staring out the kitchen window, which overlooks the backyard and the bayou. Also, often our cat would meow and move back and forth in front of one of the living room doorways, all the while looking up as if at a person who was blocking her way.

I later learned that Captain B had fallen ill during his last few years and had been confined to the house. I can only surmise that he wandered around the lower floor, watching out the front window for guests and out the back at the tributary of his beloved waterway.

The Captain seemed completely oblivious to us, like a faint residue, and indeed, he has faded considerably during the years we've lived in the house. And after I made renovations to the living room, he seemed, for a time, to vanish completely.

Three other spirits that we know about have occupied our home at some point, though two of them have not been perceived in a long time. One of these was BD, so named because he specified those initials on the Ouija Board, not only to my daughters but to some of their friends who didn't know about him. He seemed to be in his mid twenties. Mariko occasionally felt his touch, which was quite cold, and he could bend the flames of candles lit in the girls' bedrooms. BD, too, began to fade after a few years, and Mariko said he's no longer around.

A more durable spirit was a little girl, whose apparent age was six or seven. This particular spirit was confined almost solely to Sydney's room, though she occasionally entered Mariko's. I have never experienced this girl, but Sydney tells me that she is conscious of living persons occupying her space. To catch Sydney's attention, the little girl moved very light-weight objects, scooting, for example, empty plastic bags across the floor. Apparently, the little girl is shy, but one thing became certain before she eventually faded: She was terrified of Smiley.

I first became aware of Smiley about the time I started noticing the Captain. I say "became aware" because, initially, I didn't actually see him. I'd be working at my computer in the office, when I'd catch a flicker of movement out of the corner of my eye, right where the boarded-up door was. This began to occur with greater frequency—maybe twice a day. Enough that I started seeking a reason. And the more it happened, the more I became aware that, each time, I'd feel a presence move around behind me before it went through the door that led into a small hallway and the rest of the house.

The presence didn't feel very nice. It had a sort of nasty, furtive glee about it, as if it was cognizant of my discomfort and was happy to increase it. It followed a specific pattern of movement or, perhaps, simply lurked in some areas of the house but not others. It would enter through the boarded-up door and go around behind me, sometimes pausing there a few moments to try to creep me out. Then it would disappear through the door into the hallway. I didn't know where it went after that, and I never noticed its presence anywhere else in the house.

This went on for a couple of years, along with other, mostly aural, manifestations, such as the sound of footsteps walking the upstairs hall. Once, after I was well into home renovations on the place, I came home from a longish trip out of town. It was late afternoon, and the house was empty when I got home. I came in, put my luggage in the bedroom, then went into the living room to sit on the sofa and rest for a few minutes. No sooner had I sat down, than the air was filled with a multitude of creaking, popping, and bumping sounds. Multiple sounds came all at once from all over the house, and they went on for more than five minutes, gradually subsiding over the course of the next ten minutes. The house seemed almost like a dog joyfully bouncing around a returning owner, and I had the distinct sensation that it was glad I'd returned to continue fixing it up.

Not wanting to make my family uncomfortable, I didn't mention any of this to them, not realizing that both my daughters had become quite aware of Smiley on their own.

Then one day, I was sitting at my computer but hadn't yet turned it on, so the dark screen was like a dim mirror. I caught Smiley's furtive entrance out of the corner of my eye, but this time I didn't turn to try to follow it. Instead, my eyes were riveted to the computer screen because I could actually see Smiley mirrored there, creeping around behind me and heading toward the hall door.

At first glance, his tousled shock of dark hair made him look like a skinny boy in his late teens or early twenties, but he actually seems much older—from his mid thirties to his mid forties. Later, Mariko told me she thinks he's forty or so, the illusion of youth imparted by his short to medium height, slight build, and the way he crept like a ghoul or haunt in a classic horror film. He was wearing black trousers that may have been jeans and a dark gray T-shirt.

As Smiley crept around behind me, he was hunched over and taking exaggerated tiptoe steps, and his hands were held out in front of him like bony, clutching, hooked claws. It was just the sort of creeping gait that a teenage boy might use to frighten his younger sister. His mouth was pulled back in a hugely distended, horrible, and nasty grin reminiscent of the main character in the movie *Mr. Sardonicus*, and his dark, overly bright eyes were looking right at me!

I wasn't frightened, exactly, though a chill did tingle my spine. For one thing, he'd sneaked around behind me too often for me to be particularly disturbed. Though the fiendish glee gouged across his face did take me aback, after a moment, it seemed a little too theatrical. But the overall impression he projected was pretty creepy.

As he disappeared through the doorway to the hall, I thought: What a nasty fellow. He obviously delights in scaring people.

A few months passed. During that time, I never saw Smiley directly, though I occasionally caught brief glimpses of him reflected in my computer screen. Then one day, both my daughters came in and said they needed to talk to me. Had I noticed anything peculiar in the house?

I told them of my experiences with Smiley and the Captain. Both were relieved that I, too, had noticed our unusual tenants. They were familiar with the Captain, and they told me about BD and the little girl in Sydney's room. But none of the three bothered them, at least not the way Smiley did.

Sydney said Smiley would hide in the hall, and when she came through the living room and turned to go up the stairs, he'd jump out at her, body hunched, hands hooked, and that fiendish grin smearing his face, and chase her up the stairs, clutching at her with those hooked fingers. Not that she could see him at those moments, but Smiley has a very strong and visceral presence. But she *had* seen him once, reflected fairly clearly—if only momentarily—in the upstairs bathroom mirror. Her description of his appearance jibed with mine, right down to his clothes, the shock of dark hair, the fiendish grin, and the hooked, bony-fingered hands.

While Mariko never noticed him jumping out at her, she often felt him creeping up the stairs behind her. At the top of the stairs, Mariko could hurry into her room, shut the door, and be safe, because Smiley never seemed to come in but would simply hover in the hall outside her door.

For Sydney, it was a different story. Smiley would enter her room, though he seemed confined to the corner right by the door. Hidden by the door when it's open is a short, cupboard-like doorway that leads into a small storage attic, and Smiley would disappear through that. Later, during my renovations of the house, I found a cache of old boy toys—a couple of small metal cars, green plastic army men, and insect-eaten baseball cards —hidden in a nook in a back corner there.

Sometimes, when Sydney was in her room, she'd sense Smiley come in and pause before going into the storage attic. During those times, the little girl spirit would either cower behind Sydney, begging for protection, or hide in Sydney's closet. On one occasion, Sydney woke in the middle of the night and heard a sound like footsteps stomping on her floor, and then the bed began to shake back and forth. She knew who the culprit was.

Even Mariko wasn't completely safe in her room. Her bed also shook on occasion, and that continued to happen every few months for a couple of years. One night, she was talking on the phone to a person who claimed to be psychic. This person lived in Upstate New York and had never been to Houston, much less to our house, yet he accurately described its interior, the arrangement and color of the rooms, and the placement of furniture. He even mentioned that the front door had a wreath, though it wasn't Christmas. My wife had a decoration on the door that resembled a wreath.

The friend sensed BD, but Smiley was the focus of his attention. He tried to talk to Smiley, but he said that Smiley wouldn't talk to him and only mumbled sullenly in reply to his questions. Apparently, Smiley didn't appreciate the attempted contact because he immediately knocked numerous books from the bookshelves in the upstairs hall, pounded on the bedroom doors, and made the telephone answering machine in the hall go haywire, turning it on and off and causing it to beep and play messages at random.

After comparing experiences, we agreed that the Captain, BD, and the little girl were ghosts confined to their respective spaces. Smiley, however, seems to be something else. I speculated that he might be a poltergeist, considering the ages of my two daughters at the time, but Smiley has proved more durable and well traveled than the average poltergeist.

Although Smiley has a favorite pattern of movement through our house—he generally comes in the boarded-up door, goes around my desk and into the hall, then up the stairs and into Sydney's room, where he disappears into the storage attic—he has been sensed elsewhere, most frequently in the yard on the east side of the house, which is the side onto which the boarded-up door opens.

We talked to Julie about our experiences, but she'd had absolutely no inkling of Smiley's presence or of the presence of the other three spirits. But then, her area of the office was off Smiley's usual path and behind a partition of filing cabinets, and she never spent much time on the staircase or in the upstairs bedrooms or bathroom, so there was no reason for her to have encountered him.

Breaking the ice and talking about Smiley made him an open topic of discussion, and oddly, his behavior became a bit less sinister, as if dampened by our frank appraisal of him. I was of the opinion that Smiley isn't especially dangerous, though he is a nasty fellow who likes to creep out people.

My daughters were more unsettled by him. Mariko, in particular, believed that he'd be dangerous if he could interact with us on a more physical level. And she believed that he has a certain power of suggestion and that he sometimes "whispered" to her, trying to get her to harm herself or others. This suggests that he is a more ominous character than I give him credit for and reminds me of another sinister entity that I encountered when I was in my twenties. (The "Haunted: No. 10," story previously in this book.)

Another of Smiley's peculiarities seems to indicate that he isn't a ghost but some other sort of entity. Unlike the Captain, BD, and the little girl, who seemed to be inhabitants of the house, Smiley frequently disappears for periods of time. In fact, there were long stretches during the next few years that Smiley would be entirely absent or make only occasional raids on our house. And then he'd be there in full force for weeks at a time, making daily incursions.

Both my daughters had the impression that our house isn't the only place in the neighborhood that Smiley visits—that he has a regular route he follows beyond our property and into the surrounding neighborhood. This idea remained pure speculation for several years, but subsequent incidents reinforced it for us. In the first, Mariko had mentioned to her then-boyfriend, Ronnie, that we had various spirits in our house, but she'd never described them or detailed Smiley's behavior, description, or movements.

Even so, Ronnie had his own encounter with Smiley after he developed an interest in American Indian culture and had been studying it. One night, while he was in his living room at home—a mile or two from our house—he looked up to see a slightly built, hunched-over, dark-haired man enter through one of the doors and look right at him. The figure had a fiendish grin and bony, hooked fingers. It wore a feathered Indian headdress, and it was performing a patently fake Indian dance, as if mocking Ronnie. Ronnie saw this for several seconds, then the figure vanished. Smiley didn't returned to Ronnie's house after this episode—at least not so obviously—but Ronnie later sensed him at our house.

Over the years, other information on Smiley and the Captain came in. A young neighbor named Sandi Trojanowski had lost her job and moved back in with her parents, who are long-time area residents. Sandi grew up in their house, which is two doors down from ours and was built about the same time. Julie hired her to work at the dog daycare business Julie manages, and in the beginning, because Sandi wasn't then in good financial shape, Julie often gave her a ride to work.

During one of those rides, Julie asked Sandi how she liked living with her parents again, and Sandi responded that she didn't, but not because of her parents. Then she reluctantly admitted that she'd been repeatedly disturbed by a ghost or spirit when she'd lived there as a teenager. I asked Sandi what had happened to her.

Sandi's account:

"The summer before I turned seventeen, my brother, Philip, and I had bedrooms upstairs. But the weather was really hot, and we couldn't cool them enough, so we moved downstairs. There wasn't bedroom space down there, so we slept on single beds in the living room. I never had any problems while I was upstairs. I don't know what was different. But I woke up one night thinking somebody had come in the house and sat down on my bed.

"I started screaming and woke everybody up. My dad looked around the house, and there was no way anybody was in there. But when it happened again, I opened my eyes, and there was nothing there. It sat down on the end of the bed, and I could feel the pressure of it sitting. I don't remember how long it took me to do anything but just be terrified.

"We eventually had our own bedrooms downstairs, but moving into another room didn't matter. This thing sat on the end of my bed for years. At some point, I'd be scared and would put my feet over where it was going, but that was no good because the feeling would move closer to me, and I didn't want that, so I'd just scoot over and say, 'Okay, you can stay right there.'

"I would go without sleep for days. It would just keep me awake. I wondered about it, and I'd try to think of questions to ask it, then I'd go the other way and ignore it. I remember times when I'd be lying there, and I'd feel it sitting on the end of the bed, and sometimes it would be trying to get my attention. I don't want to say it was malicious, but it was impish at the very least.

"I'd try to question it. I asked it, 'Are you my grandmother? Bounce one time for yes or two times for no.' Well, then I'd get one, then, ha-ha, two! It happened for years and years of my life. All the time I was in my parents' house. Sometimes I tried to drive it away by saying, 'Get thee behind me, Satan,' or reciting the 'Prayer of St. Michael,' but nothing worked.

"It also happened when I fell asleep on the couch. It happened all over the downstairs. I moved out briefly on a couple of occasions, but I mostly lived with Mom and Dad until I was twenty-six or twenty-seven, and it never stopped happening.

"I got to where I cared less, but it never stopped scaring me, and it wouldn't leave me alone. Even when I didn't live there but would visit and fall asleep on the couch, it would happen. I worried that something was wrong with me. Why would something like that be drawn to me? But I did get better at dealing with it.

"When I lost my job and had to move back in when I was in my thirties, my cats were with me, and it never happened when they were in the bedroom with me while I slept. But if they weren't with me, it did. The cats scaring it away gave me confidence. I talked to a friend about it, and he said, 'Dogs guard your body, but cats guard your soul.' That made me feel better.

"Mom said it's happened to her since then. When it first started happening to me, I don't know that she was skeptical, but she seemed to me at the time to be pretty hard-hearted. She'd say, 'Just tell it to get the hell off your bed.' I was never scared to tell my parents about it. Mom's attitude was, 'So what? Just tell it to get off.'

"So, when it's happened to Mom since then, that's exactly what she says: 'Just get the hell off my bed, and leave me alone.' I don't know what Dad really thinks, but it's not like him to believe in something like that. He never accused me of making it up, though.

"It seemed to happen every night—or five nights a week, say. It got to the point where if it didn't happen, I say, 'Oh, my gosh. Where is it?' Then I'd think, 'You'd better stop thinking that, or it's going to come back.' If it didn't happen on any given night, I'd be shocked and count myself lucky.

"I can't pinpoint the exact time it stopped, but it definitely stopped when I moved briefly to Iowa in 2000. After I moved back, it resumed, but a lot less—something like once every week or two.

"It was really hard to believe that it was anything but malignant. I can't overstate how terrified I was when this happened. After a while, it seemed more like a poltergeist or trickster. I did also have small things that belonged to me, like pieces of jewelry, that would disappear and get moved around.

"After a while, I got the idea that it was just attention seeking. Just wanting to make a connection. I took a philosophy courses at San Jacinto Junior College, and I was talking about it to a classmate, and he asked if I'd ever thought about putting my arms around it. I said, 'Oh, no! I don't want to encourage it to stay.' It seems to like young girls. It doesn't seem to bother my mom at all.

"I never saw it, though I wondered what it might look like. Why can I not have some sense of what it is? I asked it to show itself, but it always gave ambiguous answers. In my mind, I saw it looking like the green ghost from *Ghostbusters*. I imagine it had to have a butt since it was sitting down."

Since Sandi mentioned that her mother, Kitty, had experiences with the ghost/entity, I asked Kitty about what had happened to her.

Kitty's account:

"When we were moving in many years ago, a neighbor's son, who was about twelve, rode up on a bicycle and told me, 'You know that house is haunted, don't you?' So I knew from the beginning. I prefer to call them spirits rather than ghosts. It just sounds better. And many I've encountered aren't bad, anyway.

"But in our house, it was Sandi who suffered most. She was young, and I think the spirit just wanted to pick on her.

"Nothing ever happened to me until Sandi moved out. Except for noises. People walking upstairs when nobody was there. That sort of thing has happened all the time we've lived there. After Sandi moved out, they/he/she started picking on me. But I wasn't scared. It was always the same thing. And it happened just a couple of weeks ago. I'd be in bed, almost asleep but not quite, and one part of the bed would sink down. And I'd just slap my hand over it and say, 'Get out of here. I'm going to sleep.' And whatever it was would leave and wouldn't bother me again that night.

"I do have a lot of bad dreams, and have for years, and I always wondered if somehow that's connected. And I'd hear bumping on walls. Stuff like that. It doesn't drive me crazy or anything, but it's always noises that don't seem normal. I don't really fear them, although Sandi sure did. I always figured I had the power to tell them to get out. I never heard any vocal phenomena. It sitting down on the bed is the creepiest thing."

There's no direct indication that Smiley is the same spirit responsible for the manifestations at the Trojanowskis' house, but it it interesting that occurrences of Smiley at our house increased in about 2000, the same time that Sandi's troubles decreased. In addition, in 2000, my daughters were nearing the same age that Sandi was when the spirit that troubled her began its visits.

Finally, there are clues that Smiley—or his ilk—might not be limited to our immediate area. After the original appearance of this article (which ended before the material from Sandi and Kitty Trojanowski), I received a letter from a man living in California. He told me that when he was a boy, he'd had experiences with a similar entity with a fiendish grin and hooked fingers who visited him in the night and lurked about his room.

And even more recently, I've seen that there is a phenomenon called the Grinning Man that has been seen/experienced by many people. The Grinning Man, dressed in many types of clothes, always has a manic and sardonic ear-to-ear grin, and most people who have experienced it have felt a nastiness emanating from it. And, according to Sydney, there was an episode of *Buffy the Vampire Slayer*, titled "Hush" that featured a group of similar figures. Some link the Grinning Man to aliens and UFOs, but I'm more in the camp that associates it with Shadow People, of which there are several types.

I tend to agree with Sandi that it likes to frighten young people, especially girls, but it gets as little satisfaction from Julie or me as it does from Kitty. In fact, on one rare instance that Julie perceived Smiley's presence lurking behind her, she asked it, "Why is it you never bother me." In her head, she heard the distinct reply, "Because Aunt Teet protects you." Aunt Teet was Julie's great aunt, a strong-willed black woman from Louisiana who radiated a sense of inner power right up until her death at ninety-two.

Periodically, I'll catch Smiley's movements out of the corner of my eye and sense his presence, which often is accompanied by rustling sounds and creaking floorboards right where the visual phenomenon is located. I almost always say, "Hi" or "I know you're there." He never responds, but on rare occasions, he has actually vocalized a word or two. The best such instance was when he uttered a loud, masculine, and completely sarcastic, "Ha-ha," right in my ear when I made a foolish mistake. I was on the stairs at the time. And I still frequently hear distinct footsteps in the upstairs hall and other bumping and knocking noises from various places around the house. As happened with Sandi, small objects around our house sometimes disappear, only to later reappear elsewhere.

Recently, we've also had another visitation from the Captain. During my home renovations, I opened a section of wall that had originally been a doorway between the kitchen and the adjacent room when the house was young—back when Captain B resided there. The very next day, Julie's sisters, Von and Nina, paid a visit. Neither Julie nor I had ever told either of them about the spirits in our house. For a time, the three of them sat in the living room, talking, with Julie's and Von's backs to the door to the kitchen and Nina facing it. Abruptly, Nina's eyes shifted to the doorway, then she looked at Julie and asked, "Who's that old man with the beard?"

She'd clearly seen an old man with a beard pass the doorway as if he was going across the kitchen then out the back door.

"That's the Captain," Julie replied with a smile.

The world, it would appear, is filled with various types of non-corporeal entities. Some may be lingering spirits of the deceased, some shadows of the past, and some beings with awareness, will, and the ability to interact with those of us living in three-dimensional space. Whatever Smiley might be, he was for my daughters an unwelcome presence, and they wouldn't have minded in the least if he'd never returned from one of his periodic jaunts away from our house.

They've moved on, as grown children do, but Smiley still visits on occasion, hangs around for a day or two or three, then he's gone again for a couple of months. As usual, he doesn't bother me much, though I can tell when he's here. I consider him to be a somewhat amusing puzzle rather than a threat, and to tell the truth, I'd probably miss him if he ceased to visit.

Part III
Powerful and Unseen

The Big Eye

MY TWO ROOMMATES AND I were living in a middle-class house in a middle-class neighborhood in Houston, just inside the 610 Loop at the Southwest Freeway. The neighbors didn't like us because we were three single bohemian guys disturbing their middle-class equilibrium, though really, we weren't noisy or bothersome. If they only knew what lurked just a few miles to the east, in the skyscrapers of downtown, our danger to their way of life might have paled in comparison.

To be fair, I didn't know, either, and probably few people do. And the little I can tell you, I discovered only through the agency of LSD, and what do the words of a drug-addled bohemian mean? Perhaps nothing, but I'll tell you anyway.

I was home alone, and I'd dropped the acid around mid-evening. At one point well into the trip—one or so in the morning—I was lying on my left side on my bed, and I raised my right hand and began swinging it around in a circle above me. What I was doing at first was watching the tracers chase my hand. For those who don't know, tracers are one type of visual distortion of movement that occurs to a person under the influence of a psychedelic drug. An object that moves fairly rapidly seems to leave a trail of images of itself, in decreasing clarity, as it moves. The phenomenon is related, I think, to persistence of vision, and one often sees similar visual effects used in movies, such as *The Matrix*. So, while I moved my hand, behind it followed a succession of fainter and fainter hands, all overlapping, for maybe eighteen inches behind my real hand.

I played with the effect, trying to move my hand at such a speed and in a circle of such a diameter that my real hand would overlap the final faintest image at the end of the trail, creating an unbroken circle. It was all just a game until I noticed that, when I did achieve the circle and had kept it going for a short time, the circular movement of my hand was creating a vortex in the air, much as it would have created the beginnings of a whirlpool had I been stirring my hand around in a tub of water.

The substance of this vortex was not the air itself, although that, too, may have been mildly affected, but rather some subtle substance that permeated the air. I have since come to understand that this substance is the field of universal chi that pervades everything, but it was just a curious phenomenon to me at the time.

As I played with the vortex, I found that the faster I stirred, the higher it climbed into the room. I got it going all the way to the ceiling, and it was like a little gray tornado, with my shoulder at its lowest point. Curious, I spun a little harder, and the top of the tornado lifted through the ceiling and out of the roof. In just a few minutes, I had the vortex spinning some fifty or sixty feet in the air above the house. It was a narrow funnel, and the diameter at its mouth was maybe six or eight feet.

I wasn't thinking of possible uses for this energy but was just having fun playing with it—I was like some cosmic cowboy with a magic lasso that just begged to be whirled and spun. Interestingly, the lasso seemed to be an amplified part of my own energy, and as it rose above the house, it carried my personal awareness with it.

Though it was nighttime, I could see all around over the rooftops of my neighborhood and farther away. The landscape was gray and dimly lit, as it would have been on a very gray and hazy day, and the buildings downtown, several miles to the northeast, were apparent as a darker gray mass in which a few individual architectural lines could be made out. It looked something like a modernist, fog-shrouded cityscape. I'd "seen" this way before, as told in the story of the Burnet Experience related earlier in this book, so I was not surprised but simply took the phenomenon for granted.

Suddenly, in the midst of my exhilaration, I saw something flash atop one of the taller buildings downtown. Flash isn't really the right word—what I saw was a momentary but bright flare of energy that wasn't light. It caught my notice, and as I stared that way, the flare appeared several more times at gradually decreasing intervals. It wasn't a random blaze of undirected energy but more like a searchlight that speared out and swept back and forth across the landscape, and the apparent flaring happened when its aim passed my location, though, again, it wasn't composed of light. Instead, it was a blaze of profoundly powerful attention.

Each time this blaze of attention passed across me, I could feel the pressure of a concentrated, scouring awareness. I wasn't seeing a projected illumination, but an intense and powerful psychic vision that was scanning the city. I began to think of it as the Big Eye, something akin to Sauron's Orb that sought out Frodo in J.R.R. Tolkien's *Lord of the Rings* trilogy. Only this wasn't fiction, but real. As its vision swept back and forth across the landscape in rapidly decreasing arcs, I could tell that it was narrowing its range of focus as it zeroed in on something it was looking for. Something that had disturbed its awareness.

With a shock, I realized that I was at the center of its narrowing swing! The Big Eye was looking for me!

My lasso of energy was powerful enough—or at least visible enough—to disrupt the energy field in this part of the city, attracting the attention of someone, or something, that could detect fluctuations in this field. I was like a bug that had run out in the middle of the floor, waving a flag that advertised its presence. Whatever it was that resided at the top of one of the downtown skyscrapers wanted to know what little mite had the temerity to think it could dare attempt to magically manipulate reality within its range of perception and power.

In the instant that I felt all this, my magical lasso, formerly such bold fun, now was a rather puny and a completely unwanted ensign of identity and location. I knew the Big Eye hadn't quite yet pinpointed me and that if I was careful, it wouldn't know exactly where, or who, I was. I immediately stopped swinging my arm, the lasso of energy retracted into me, and I lay as quietly and as still on the bed as I could.

Perhaps I was unduly paranoid. Though I thought I detected malevolence in the gaze of the Big Eye, maybe what I really felt was just the imponderable weight of power, knowledge, and implacability that were well beyond me.

I sometimes wonder what would have happened if I had I kept the lasso going—not as a challenge but as a man adrift signals a passing ship that can rescue him from watery oblivion. I think, though, that I probably was wiser to hide. After all, one does not mess with someone who might be akin to the Lord of Mordor. Whatever was up there on the top of that building, it had far too much power for me to simply stand up and brazenly shout my position and invite myself to be ground like a bug under heel.

Now, these many years later, I wonder if that Big Eye still blazes like a beacon downtown. And who, or what, is doing the looking?

Channel One

I FIRST MET MARJORIE KERR in fall 1984. A short brunette in her mid thirties, she was one of a small group who gathered weekly at the church where I taught tai chi chuan, the Chinese physical and mental exercise and martial art. Because Margie came to practice directly after work, she usually arrived half an hour before the rest of the class, and we'd spend the time chatting. As the months passed, we felt a growing bond of friendship, and I learned that she was a talented palmist a well as a trained hypnotherapist who often dealt with past life phenomena.

But things changed, as they must, and Margie had to stop her lessons. Though we continued to have contact, it was not on a regular basis. During these months, Margie quit her daytime job to devote full time to her hypnotherapy practice. Then, early in spring 1985, she met a woman experienced in channeling—one type of the various phenomena that used to be grouped under the label of mediumship. Margie's association with the woman led to training, and the natural talent, sensitivity, and empathy that made Margie such a good palmist and hypnotherapist resulted in her becoming a channel for several multi-dimensional beings.

During the training, Margie experienced only a light trance state and minimal contact with the beings. Her first major breakthrough came a few weeks after the training. She was talking on the telephone to a close friend, Gary, when, as she described it, someone just "stepped in and pushed me aside." A voice that wasn't hers began speaking to Gary. He knew Margie had gone through the training, and though he was startled at first, he quickly realized what was happening. The next few times Margie channeled, much the same sort of thing occurred. She would suddenly find herself displaced as one of the beings spoke through her. During these early incidents, the channel was unclear, as if cluttered with psychic static.

Soon, however, the channel cleared up somewhat, and Margie discovered she could open the channel voluntarily. After that, the beings did not take the initiative, but let her do so. A couple of months passed, during which the channeling sessions drained Margie considerably, causing disorientation, exhaustion, and nausea. The beings told listeners that there was interference due to an inexact complement of vibratory rates between Margie and themselves. Then the main being, named Elena, said she was going to make an adjustment. After that, the channel was much clearer, and the sessions became less debilitating for Margie. Though she still felt drained and disoriented, particularly after sessions lasting an hour or more, the nausea disappeared.

Throughout spring 1985, Margie channeled for two groups of people. The first, and larger, group was open to anyone who wished to attend. In these sessions, people asked questions pertaining to personal spirituality and difficulties as well as general and specific questions about the world at large and the nature of reality. The second, smaller, group consisted of two or three of Margie's close friends and was more in the nature of friendly get-togethers during which the entities behaved less formally.

There were two primary entities who channeled through Margie. First was Elena. Elena could be described as a being of high order. She spoke, she said, through thousands of channels on this planet and, apparently, on others. She manifested in many different ways, depending on the channel she used. Through Margie, she manifested as female, firm but gentle and somewhat remote but not unfriendly. She always looked to higher purposes and, even while answering the most direct of questions, would preface her answer with technical or philosophical background. A gently ironic sense of humor emerged as long as the listener paid attention. If the listener's attention wandered, however, she became serious.

Her manner of speech was careful and deliberate, and she distinctly enunciated each word. This gave a slightly mechanical effect to her tone, though her speech was not unfeeling. Elena tended toward the matter-of-fact in approach and the factual in content. What she said always seemed to stretch the bounds of the listener and had meaningful content for every person present, no matter to whom she directed her speech. She was, apparently, the "leader" of the beings that channeled through Margie. She always used the pronoun "we" instead of "I."

The second major entity was Carl. Closer to the human plane of existence than was Elena, he was a bit more earthy and companionable in manner. His information tended to deal with relationships, guidance in exercise and health, and other practical aspects of life. He spoke through only a handful of channels and almost seemed to be a sort of trainee whose supervisor was Elena. Once, while he was talking, the listeners asked for Elena. He said he couldn't find her right then, for she was busy somewhere else. The listeners asked what was happening. "It's something big, but I'm not sure what," Carl replied, humor in his voice. "They never tell me what's going on." He said his link with Margie had a lot to do with aiding her study and practice of psychology because that was his specialty. His speech flowed more smoothly than Elena's, and he was apt to joke more than she. He sometimes used "I" as well as "we."

There were several other beings of lesser importance. One was Tanya, who seemed to be linked somehow with Carl. Margie described her as a caricature of a breathy blond bombshell out of a James Bond movie. Another was Maria. Her dimension was similar to our conception of the world of fairies, elves, and plant spirits. Sometimes her world approached close to ours, and at others it was farther away. She often came through during the time of the full moon. She had a light personality with a childlike innocence, and she talked mostly about plant life and water. There were a few others who came through once or twice.

I hadn't had an opportunity to attend any of the channeling sessions though I'd wanted to. Personal concerns and a busy schedule kept me away. In April, Margie resumed her tai chi lessons, which, because of circumstance, I taught privately at her home. May and the first two weeks of June were unusually hot and dry, but the weather finally broke on Tuesday, June 11, when a strong thunderstorm blew across Houston. The storm dumped a lot of badly needed water and was accompanied by extensive atmospheric electrical activity.

The following Friday, I arrived in the morning for Margie's lesson. We talked about inconsequential matters for a few minutes then went outside for her lesson. After working for an hour, we came back into the apartment, which occupied the bottom floor of a two-story house. The house sits on a corner lot that faces a fairly busy street. Once inside, Margie told me that, on the day of the storm, a considerable amount of paranormal activity had occurred in her house. Immediately interested, I asked for details. The story she told was both frightening and puzzling.

Margie's first indication that something was wrong came with the odd behavior of her dog, Rafki. Rafki was a hundred-and-twenty-pound Rhodesian Ridgeback, a type of dog bred for hunting and killing lions. They are tenacious, powerful, and brave, and Rafki, now well into middle age, was normally fearless when it came to tangible dangers. But all afternoon, he'd been acting strangely: fearful and nervous. Margie didn't pay much attention to Rafki's behavior, though. She'd had a busy day, and that evening, she was going to visit a friend,

Bill. Feeling centered and in a good mood despite the storm outside, she headed for the shower.

As she stepped under the water, though, the good mood was jolted away by a sudden image of being electrocuted while in the shower. She pushed the unusual thought away, but it came back. She tried to ignore it, but within moments, she was overcome by a powerful sense of fear and danger accompanied by the impression that someone was standing on the other side of the shower curtain.

To her horror, the shower curtain began to sway back and forth. Immediately the shower scene from the movie *Psycho* flashed through her mind. She was frightened but soon calmed herself since she'd neither seen nor heard anyone—nor had Rafki, who was in the apartment with her. But even while she chalked up her thoughts and feelings to tension from her busy day, the unease persisted.

Though determined not to give in to her fears, she quickly finished her shower, left the bathroom, and stepped through the tiny hall leading to her bedroom. After dressing and blow-drying her hair, she walked back into the hall, where she happened to glance through the open door that led into the room where she practiced hypnotherapy.

Directly across the therapy room was a door that opened into another, longer hall that, in turn, led to the reception room for her therapy practice. The front door to the reception room was clearly visible through the rooms and hall from where she stood, about forty feet away. Set in the upper half of the door was a large window covered with a silver film that blocked vision while letting light enter. Startled, she saw a man's head and shoulders silhouetted on the window.

Her immediate thought was that a friend was outside and had been knocking, which she hadn't heard because of the hair dryer. It was odd he'd come to her business entrance rather than to the separate front door that led to her private living space. Feeling no fear but worried he might leave before she could get to the door, she hurried through the therapy room, down the hall, and across the reception room, still seeing the silhouetted head and shoulders. But when she flung open the door, the front porch was empty!

Baffled, she looked around but saw no one. Then suddenly, an inexplicable terror hit her, for it seemed as if the pressure of an unseen presence or force entered when she opened the door. Closing and locking the door, she turned around. Horrified, she discovered that the atmosphere in the reception room, the hall, and particularly the therapy room seemed thick and viscous with a sort of whitish taint that wasn't smoke. Menace suffused everything.

Filled with fear, she picked up the phone in the reception room and dialed Gary's number because he was familiar with her channeling experiences. After hearing the story, he advised her to leave and invited her over to his home. She told him she was already expected at Bill's, but she'd call later to let him know she'd arrived safely. Then Margie hung up and proceeded to leave.

Without returning to her bedroom or passing through the therapy room, she went through the dining room, which is situated off the main hall, between the living room toward the front and the kitchen toward the back. Rafki, whose terror had increased during the entire episode, followed her as she hurried though the kitchen to the back door.

Seeing he was frightened of what was occurring in the apartment, Margie called for him to come with her, yet fearful as he was, he was even more afraid of the lightning and thunder outside. Try as she might, Margie couldn't coax him out into the storm. Feeling that he was not in danger, she left him.

She locked the back door, splashed through the rain to the carport, got in her car, and left. When she arrived at Bill's, she phoned Gary to let him know she was all right. He told her to come over to his place to spend the night if she felt she needed to. After hanging up, she sat with Bill on the couch and related the events of the evening. Bill listened and calmed her down.

Even though she now felt physically safe, she began to feel her energy was being pulled back to her apartment. She had the sensation of the couch elongating, until Bill seemed very far away. Perceiving the need to enter an altered state of consciousness and follow the energy's pull, she instructed Bill to allow her no more than ten or fifteen minutes in trance. She lay down, and almost immediately, her consciousness descended into a dreamlike realm where she experienced a number of horrifying visions.

Margie's spirit was drawn back to her apartment, then to the earth beneath it, where she saw strips of human flesh being charred over an open fire for consumption. Large quantities of grease and blood from the strips dripped down to soak into the ground. Then her consciousness moved into the earth itself. The consistency of the earth was strange, with an unpleasant, viscous, black, shiny stuff mixed in it. Going deeper, she passed through a level composed of many kinds of animal entrails. There were strong feelings of black magic, sacrifice, and evil that permeated these perceptions.

Deeper and deeper she went, leaving the viscous black layer and animal remains behind. A vista opened before her of a white stone temple. She noticed she was in a different body, though still female. As she approached the temple, she was captured by guards, who took her to an altar where she was to be sacrificed. Moments before the sacrifice occurred, she woke up in another body, that of a woman living in Victorian England. The woman had been sleeping with her husband, and she promptly woke him and related the hideous dream of being sacrificed she'd just had.

Then this scene, too, faded, and Margie began moving up through the earth. She passed through the layer of animal remains, through the viscous, black stuff, through the fire with its strips of charring flesh, then back into her body in Bill's apartment. About fifteen minutes had passed since she entered the trance state. Bill said that at times during her trance, Margie actually looked like different people. She had trembled, and several times her body had curiously bloated then deflated.

Margie remained at Bill's for several hours, after which she reluctantly returned to her apartment. Both the back screen and door opened without problem, and just inside, Rafki was waiting for her, still in a state of fear. Sensing that the strangeness in the apartment was still present, though dissipated, Margie decided to check out the place. The feeling of terror she previously experienced was absent as she moved cautiously from room to room. The living room and the reception room were fairly "clean," but as she was about to step into the therapy room, she stopped stock still.

The atmosphere still held some of the smoky thickness it had manifested before she'd left, and the air was alive with electricity, with small tongues of lightning licking and snapping here and there.

At first she thought her eyes were playing tricks, but as she watched, she realized she was actually seeing electric sparks discharge in the room. Stunned, she stepped back. Knowing she wasn't about to sleep in the apartment, she decided to accept Gary's offer of shelter for the night. She wanted to get a nightgown and change of clothes from her bedroom, but that would have meant crossing the therapy room. Deciding she didn't want the nightgown badly enough to pass through a miniature lightning storm, she returned to the back door. This time, though the storm outside was still active, Rafki was all too happy to go with her.

Oddly, Margie had a very difficult time getting her door shut. She had been in the apartment less than five minutes, and the door had opened readily enough when she'd entered, but now it took all of her strength to close it. Then the lock wouldn't work. After struggling with it for several minutes, she finally managed to turn the key. Even the screen door wouldn't shut properly. Then she and Rafki got into her car, and she drove to Gary's.

When she arrived, Margie filled in Gary on what had transpired since she'd last talked to him. She tried to go into a trance so Gary could speak with Elena but was unable to open the channel. She said it felt as if she was disconnected.

The following day, she returned to her apartment. Foreboding still seemed to linger in the air, though much diminished from the night before. Nor did she experience any further overt phenomena, such as seeing the silhouetted figure at the front door or the lightning storm in the therapy room. The back door again worked properly.

Even so, she remained uneasy throughout the day. That evening, with Gary present, she tried to open the channel, and this time, she managed to get through.

Elena answered, and Gary asked her about the disturbances. Elena told him that several factors contributed to Margie's difficulties. Foremost among them were metallic deposits in the area and a nearby geophysical formation. Elena specified that the major metals in the deposits were iron, copper, and zinc, though others were present. The nature of the geophysical formation was unidentified. She also stated that other factors influenced the situation, but she did not elaborate.

As to the nature of the disturbances, Elena stated that they were not the result of evil but of strong earth and other energies that centered in that geographical area. These energies were intensely antagonistic to the energies of Margie's personal makeup, which was why Margie had perceived them as being evil. And last, Elena advised Margie to move from her apartment.

After hearing Margie's tale, my curiosity was aroused, and I questioned her. As one might expect of any psychically sensitive person, Margie had had many experiences of a paranormal sort throughout her life, though she had tended to block such occurrences during her childhood. None of them, however, quite compared to the events of the past week.

I asked about her tenure in the apartment. She'd lived in the house for nearly five years, though the first four had been spent with a roommate in the upstairs apartment. During that time, she'd never noticed anything strange about the building. Only in the last year, since moving downstairs and living by herself, had she experienced unusual incidents.

Odd happenings began occurring almost immediately. While hanging curtains in the living room, she turned on the lamp, only to have the bulb forcefully pop out of the fixture. Thinking it strange, she got another bulb and screwed it in, but again the fixture spit out the bulb. Despite this, she finished hanging the curtains but, since then, never really used the room. True, it was furnished with a comfortable couch and padded chairs, but the only time anyone sat in the room was when she had guests. As Margie talked, she recalled that the previous tenants had never used that room as a living space either, but only for storage, which was unusual considering that the front door opened directly into that room and it *was* the living room.

She also noticed a behavioral change in her dog. Rafki was nine at the time of the move and had never before shown signs of fright at thunderstorms. Now, however, he was terrified of them, having developed his fear while living in the downstairs apartment. On nights of thunder and lightning, he would literally throw himself over Margie. It was as if, having no tangible enemy to attack, he did the only thing he could, which was to defend Margie with his body.

Then there was an incident that took place before Margie became a channel. It happened in the therapy room while Margie and Gary lounged late one night on the carpeted floor, talking, as they often did. After a while, they both fell asleep. Gary woke suddenly in the early morning hours, feeling groggy and ill at ease. Rafki paced worriedly around the room. Gary looked up to see an extraordinary sight. Floating in the air was what he termed a "blue entity." As he described it, the apparition was a human-sized ellipsoid that gave off a bright but hazy blue light. It seemed that his own perception accounted for the haziness rather than any sort of blurriness inherent in the apparition.

For the few moments Gary stared at it, he felt emanating from it the most tremendous sense of power and love he'd ever experienced, and along with the power and love came a joyous recognition. Before that recognition jelled into a specific image, he turned to wake Margie and suddenly realized that his body hadn't moved. His mind was conscious, but his body was still asleep. He dragged himself fully awake and shook Margie, but she wouldn't wake. He could no longer see the blue apparition.

Apprehensive, Gary made every attempt to rouse Margie, and at last succeeded in bringing her partially to consciousness. She began mumbling imagery from a vivid, dream-like state where a group of entities were trying to convince her of the ultimate futility of her friendship with Gary. Since the friendship was doomed to eventual dissolution, they argued and she mimicked in a strange voice, the ties should be cut now. As she finally became semiconscious, the state lost its grip on her, though its influence was still strong. Both she and Gary were groggy and disoriented, but he was less affected than she.

The unconscious statements that Margie had uttered against their friendship shocked Gary, but he kept his head and attempted to rouse Margie enough so they could leave the apartment and go to his place for the night. She was difficult to awake fully and several times slipped back into the dreamlike state where the entities again maligned Gary. Mounting fear and tension laced the atmosphere, and an unusual number of creaking, thumping, and other house sounds filled the air.

Gary realized that all this was getting too weird, and he couldn't take any more.

Outside on the darkened street, a speeding van screeched to a halt as it slid around the corner where Margie's house sits. The sound galvanized Gary into action, and he pulled Margie toward the door. The van sat still for a few seconds after they emerged from the apartment, then it pulled away and roared off. Gary finally got Margie into his car, and he drove away from the scene. Before they'd gone far, the van came back by as it made a circuit of the block, then it disappeared up a side street. Once Margie was away from her apartment, the bizarre dream state dissipated, and she returned to normal consciousness. She remembered in a hazy way what she had said but couldn't account for the content.

Other strange things had happened. Frequently, Margie would hear sounds in her apartment like the movement of people. The mail slot would bang repeatedly, and loud knockings came from the front door that opened into the therapy reception room. This sounded exactly as if someone was at the door, knocking for attention, but invariably, no one was there when Margie opened the door. This is the same door at which she later saw the manlike silhouette on the window.

Gary later told me he could tell when an increase of forces in the apartment was imminent by observing Margie. He noticed that before he felt anything unusual, Margie would become groggy. By the time he was affected, she would be "out of it."

I asked which rooms in her apartment made her feel most uncomfortable. They were the living room, the reception room, the therapy room, and the main bathroom between the latter two. The back bedroom and second bathroom that adjoined the small hall directly behind the therapy room seemed to be relatively clear of influence, as were the dining room and kitchen. If you stood in front of the building, looking at it, the front and left rooms of the lower apartment were the problem areas.

As was obvious from their location and style of construction, the back bedroom and second bath were additions built more recently than the rest of the house. This surmise was strengthened by the fact that the little hall that led to the two exited only into the therapy room, which originally had been a bedroom. I requested to see the inside of the addition to be sure, speculating that if it had been constructed later, that might help explain why it wasn't affected.

Margie agreed, with the stipulation that she tidy up the room before I went in. Then she told me there was a spot in the therapy room that felt strange or different from the rest of the room. She wondered if I could find it while she straightened up the bedroom. I said I'd try, and we went to the therapy room. I paused at the threshold to gauge the sensations I felt then stepped inside.

Immediately on entering, I felt a sort of mild, electrical chill run through my body, causing the hairs on my arms and neck to prickle and tingly shivers to run up my spine. It was very similar to a continuous, extremely mild electric current. And in fact, the air in the room did seem a bit thick, though I had no difficulty moving or breathing. I told Margie that I could feel a charge of some sort in the room. She nodded, followed me into the room, then went to the hall leading to the back bedroom and bath and disappeared into the bedroom. Meanwhile, I set about finding the spot she mentioned.

The room was a normal-sized bedroom, about fourteen by sixteen feet. The center of the floor was occupied by the elevated recliner on which Margie's hypnotherapy clients would lie, but it was possible to walk around the periphery and stand in each of the four quadrants of the room without hindrance. I'd followed Margie to the entrance of the little hall, so, beginning in that corner, I stood still, noting my sensations. After a few moments, I moved to the next corner, on to the third and fourth, then back to the first.

By the time I'd gotten back to the corner I'd started in, I thought I already knew the location of the spot. It was a power spot, emanating energy

I made a second transit to be certain. Yes, the sensations were the same. In the corner where I began, I actually felt less of a charge than when I'd first entered the room. As I arrived in the second corner, however, a shivering jolt of electrical-type energy surged through soles of my feet, up my legs and torso, into my head, and down my arms to my fingertips. It felt just like the ambient energy in the room but directional and many times stronger—a flow rather than a mild field of energy. Actually, the feeling wasn't too unpleasant to me and had a sort of exciting effect, though I thought that prolonged or more intense exposure would become tiresome and even enervating.

Moving to the third corner, I felt the surge of energy dwindle. The tingling was still stronger than the general ambience but was not a definite flow as it was in the second corner. In the fourth corner, where the door I'd entered was located, it was weaker still, more on the order of the general ambience. Moving back to the first corner, I felt the energy sink to a level lower than the general ambience. To check this, I stepped forward, next to the recliner in the middle of the room, and felt the tingling energy go back up to about the level of the third corner.

I made a third circuit of the room to verify my findings, and as I finished and returned to the first corner, Margie reentered. Telling her I thought the spot was in the second corner, I walked over to it. For the fourth time, I felt the tingling surge of energy coursing through me, though as I reached the corner it suddenly seemed less than it had as I approached.

"Step back one step," Margie advised. I did, and again felt the energy in full force. I had overstepped the spot by about a foot.

Marveling at the feeling, I shuffled back and forth, left and right, attempting to define the limits and shape of the spot. It seemed to be about two feet in diameter. I could get one foot on the spot and one off and feel the energy course up only the side of my body that was over the spot. I played in the energy for a few minutes, then Margie told me she was feeling uneasy and asked if we could go out onto the front porch to talk. After I made a quick survey of the back bedroom to make certain that it was a relatively recent addition to the main structure and also was relatively free of the tingly energy, we went outside to the front porch, which was at the opposite end of the house from the therapy room.

We made ourselves comfortable on the cement steps, and I speculated on our findings thus far. In general, I ruled out recent witchcraft, black magic, or other specific evil as being responsible. The reasons for this were simple. Margie had seen the blood and melted fat from the charring strips of flesh dripping into the soil, not onto the floor, and she was firm in her belief that these impressions had come from the earth beneath the house rather than from the structure itself. Also, she'd lived in the house's second-floor apartment for several years without negative incident. Only after she'd moved to the first-floor apartment—closer to the ground the house was built on—did the disturbances begin. It was the earth beneath that was in question, not the house. This meant that if some sort of psychic residue from evil magic was involved, it had to have taken place before the structure was built.

Houston is a relatively new city, and the neighborhood where Margie's house sat was swampy forest before the present neighborhood was constructed in the early 1900s. From the architecture of her house and my knowledge of the city, I could tell that her house probably was the original structure built on that site. Of course, that didn't rule out the chance that a farmhouse had existed there before the neighborhood had sprung up, but that likelihood seemed remote. So, if the property did retain psychic residues of evil magic, the magic probably hadn't been performed by the people who'd settled the area during the days when Texas belonged to Mexico or by subsequent inhabitants.

A second possibility seemed more likely, given the grisly, cannibalistic details. Before Anglos settled Texas, the region was occupied by Indians. One of the tribes, the Karankawa, ranged along the Gulf Coast from Galveston Bay to Corpus Christi, and bands often migrated seasonally between the barrier islands and the mosquito-infested thickets inland, so it is possible that they set up one of their camps on this exact site. The point is of some importance, for the Karankawa were eaters of the flesh of enemies captured or killed in battle.

The Karankawa had a reputation for being dirty and dangerous, and as a rule, they were shunned by other regional tribes. As late as 1816, forts were built on Bolivar Peninsula, just northeast of Galveston, to protect the settlers from Karankawa raids. This is from the *Wikipedia* entry on the Karankawa:

> According to some sources, the Karankawa practiced ritual cannibalism of blood enemies, in common with other coastal tribes of Texas and Louisiana. In 1768, a Spanish priest wrote an account of the Karankawa ritual ceremonies. He portrayed the Karankawa as believing that eating the captive's flesh would transfer the captive's power and strength to those who consumed him. The natives tied a captive to a stake. While dancing around him, they would dart in, slice off a piece of flesh and roast it in front of the victim in a prepared campfire. Then they would devour it.

This definitely jibed with Margie's vision of strips of roasting human flesh. No one knows for certain where the Karankawa picked up a taste for human flesh, but one story has it that they learned cannibalism from the crew of a Spanish ship wrecked on the coast in 1528. This, again, from *Wikipedia*:

> Álvar Núñez Cabeza de Vaca, a Spanish conquistador who lived among the Karankawa for several years in the 1530s, made no mention of cannibalism. To the contrary, Cabeza de Vaca acknowledged that he and his fellow Spanish conquistadors committed acts of cannibalism on their own dead to stay alive after shipwrecking off Galveston Bay.

The Karankawa lived a poor life, and food was scarce along the desolate and often marshy coastline. The environment offered the castaway Spanish crewmen very little food, either, and legend has it that some of the members resorted to their mates when the larder was otherwise empty. The Indians witnessed this, and thinking the Spaniards returned deities, simply emulated them. It could be that the reason Cabeza de Vaca never mentions cannibalism among the Karankawa is that they took it up only after his departure.

Whatever the case may be, the Karankawa were so prone to violent attacks on their neighbors that they often came into conflict with other Indians and white men alike. Eventually, the tribe was driven out of Texas and into Mexico, where the last remaining band was annihilated in 1858. Evidence of the Karankawa's somewhat lengthy stay remains in stone points and other artifacts still to be found by visitors to Texas beaches.

Whether or not the story of the tribe learning cannibalism from the shipwrecked crew is historically accurate, it is true that the Karankawa ate human flesh, and I speculated that it was possible that Margie had tuned into psychic residue from a Karankawa cannibal feast during her descent into the earth beneath her house. But if a cannibal feast at that location was not out of the bounds of possibility, neither was it probable. Only an archaeological dig could unearth evidence that this had been a feast site, and without such evidence, all else was speculation.

So, lack of evidence, coupled with high degrees of improbability, ruled out black magic and some evil occurrence of an unspecified nature and made a cannibalistic feast possible but not necessarily likely. This coincided with Elena's statement to Gary that the disturbances were not caused by evil forces but by energies contradictory to Margie's own energies.

The visions of blood and charring flesh Margie had experienced seemed to me to be explicable in another way. If, as her channeled entities had stated, the energies of that location ran counter to Margie's personal energies, they might manifest in ways indicative of their own nature as well as in ways that would frighten Margie.

The channeled entities informed Gary that the negative energies had characteristics of fire and metal—notably iron and copper—and the primary images Margie saw had been of fire and blood united in the unpleasant and fearsome image of strips of human flesh being cooked. The image of blood saturating the earth is significant when you consider the iron content of blood, which itself, as an element of the human body, partakes particularly of heat, both in color and metaphorically. As does copper, which is the constituent metal in the blood of invertebrates.

I felt that the energies were manifesting in symbols that reflected their nature and that were, at the same time, frightening to Margie due to the antipathetic polarities involved. The same idea seemed to hold true with respect to the images Margie experienced while showering. First had been the fear of electrocution. That would be fire. Next had come the images from *Psycho*, and there's the blood and fear again. Then had been the subsequent fear caused by the menace she'd experienced when she'd opened the front door after seeing the silhouetted masculine figure—itself another

*Psycho*esque image. The menace and fear emphasized the actual possibilities inherent in the *Psycho* images.

In fact, the idea of antipathetic polarities held true for the majority of Margie's frightening experiences that night. For the thickening of the atmosphere in the apartment and the miniature electrical storm in the therapy room, I had no explanation. I did find it interesting, though, that Margie received what seemed to be a precognitive warning about electrocution while showering in the bathroom, which was adjacent to the room where, just a few hours later, she observed the electrical discharges.

Some of the other elements of the story also made tentative sense. The layer of viscous black substance that Margie traveled through could have represented an underground pool of petroleum. Such features are common beneath the plains of the Gulf Coast and also could be linked to copper deposits since petroleum is mostly composed of the bodies of billions upon billions of invertebrate organisms, whose blood, as previously noted, utilizes copper instead of iron.

I also had a couple of ideas on the geophysical formation the channeled entities had mentioned. Knowing a little about the terrain Houston is founded on, I believed that such a formation was most probably one of two kinds. Houston is notably lacking in bedrock, but it has an abundance of fault lines and underground streams.

Many of the more serious fault lines in the city are visible to the naked eye, either as minor irregularities in altitude of a few inches to a few feet, or as permanent cracks across roadbeds that city workers never can seem to fix, despite years of effort. I had not heard of any fault lines in this particular neighborhood, but I knew of more than one spot within a few blocks where underground streams had either surfaced or eaten out areas beneath roadbeds, causing small sink-holes. I thought that an underground stream might be the geophysical culprit, and that it might run diagonally beneath the house from the therapy room to the living room, accounting for the effect on only that part of the house.

Sitting on the front steps, Margie and I had taken our speculations about as far as we could. Then I suggested we go around to the side of the house, look under the therapy room, and see what we could see. In moments, we were there, on hands and knees, peering under the house. Like many of the older houses in Houston, this one had a pier-and-beam foundation, where the larger support beams rest on piers of heavy concrete blocks. In the case of Margie's house, there was about two feet of space between the ground and the floor joists.

The first thing we noted was an abundance of scrap metal lying beneath the therapy room. I dragged out an iron rod a yard long, thirty feet of old wiring, and a galvanized corrugated iron sheet that was 4'x8' but bent roughly in half lengthwise, and tossed them aside. Farther back, out of easy reach, was an ancient and rusted-out push grass mower, some old galvanized iron plumbing pipe, and other metal debris. I surveyed all the metal debris, noting that it almost entirely consisted of iron, copper, and zinc, the three metals that the channeled entities said contributed to Margie's troubles.

Then, Margie drew my attention to a peculiar mounded area about four feet under the edge of the house. The bent galvanized sheet had been lying on top of it. The mound was roughly circular and about three feet in diameter and lumped several inches higher than the surrounding soil. While the surrounding dirt was a medium to dark sepia in color, the mound had a sickly grayish tinge and was crusty looking, as if salts or too much fertilizer were dissolved in the soil.

Realizing we might have something here, I stood up and looked through the window into the therapy room. I looked back under the house, then into the therapy room again. The sickly gray mound was directly beneath the spot on the floor in the therapy room where the power surge emerged.

We knelt there for several more minutes, speculating on the location of the mound and its relationship to the galvanized metal sheet, the other metallic debris, and various water and sewer pipes nearby as well as to possible pooling patterns water might make beneath the house during a rain. Any one of these factors could, and probably did contribute to the effects of Tuesday night.

Then, as we stood and dusted off our knees, Margie asked if I would monitor a channeling session and question the entities about our speculations and findings. I agreed, and we went back into the house, where we sat on a sofa. The session was tape-recorded, and the dialog presented here is verbatim.

I was very interested not only in observing a channeling session but in actually speaking at length with the entities. And I was a little nervous that I get things right. After all, I didn't really know what to expect. As it turned out, my nervousness was misplaced. I spoke with only one of Margie's entities, but the experience was no different than conversing with a person. Margie's eyes were closed, but except for that, her features expressed a range of emotions, from the serious and intent to the humorous. Aside from its use of the plural pronoun "we" instead of the singular "I," the entity spoke directly and simply. Its intention seemed to be to aid understanding. I will hereafter to refer to it as a she because that's how she manifested through Margie, though I wonder if her gender was just a construct, rather than a true feature.

The session began when Margie made herself comfortable, leaned back, and closed her eyes. She shivered, and her body relaxed. She shivered again and relaxed further, then she shivered a third time, and her features went slack. Her body looked so relaxed that she seemed to be asleep. Then, as if waking, she sat up easily. Her eyes remained closed, but personality again fleshed out her features. Less than two minutes had passed.

"How may we assist you?" she asked.

I rapidly assessed the voice, both quality and intonation, and Margie's feeling of presence. It was obviously Margie sitting before me, but there was a feeling of another persona as well. This observation is merely subjective, of course, but often events unfold too quickly or contain influences that are too subtle to make objective measurements. Besides, sometimes subjective observation is the only observation of real importance. I knew what Margie "felt" like, and while this person in front of me was, without a doubt, Margie, there seemed to be someone else there as well.

The voice did not sound like Margie's usual speaking voice—it was a bit higher and lighter than Margie's—and there was no trace of accent. The deliberate intonation and impression of distance made me think, even at this early stage, that I might be talking with Elena, and I followed that assumption for the duration of the conversation.

"Hello," I replied. Elena smiled slightly and inclined her head in my direction. "I would like to ask some questions on Margie's behalf concerning the disturbances that took place here last Tuesday. I believe you were questioned the next day about the disturbances and told Gary there were several factors involved. Of those, two had the most influence: metal deposits and a geophysical structure in the earth beneath the house. Is this correct?"

"As we told Margie," Elena said, "These factors have a great influence on the energies that are the cause of the disturbances, as you call them."

Her answer immediately gave me pause. In the first place, it implied that additional factors were involved. Even more telling was her use of the phrase, "as you call them." As *I* call them. How simple, yet how difficult. Already, I'd run up against my own limitations. I called them disturbances because they seemed unnatural and because Margie had been fearful during the occurrences. In reality, though, they were simply among the natural order of things and not "disturbances" at all. And as the conversation progressed, I had to confront further limitations to my thinking. For the time being, I realized, I was going to have to think in less structured ways than was my custom.

"I'd like to know more about these metal deposits. You informed Gary that they consist primarily of iron, copper, and zinc, but that there are others."

"These are the principal metals, yes, and there are other minerals as well."

"Are these metals in chunks or are they diffused through the soil?"

"There are some large pieces beneath ground level, but most of the larger pieces are close to and on the surface and consist of what you would call human garbage."

I immediately thought of the metal junk Margie and I had found beneath the house. Most of it was iron, but the corrugated iron sheet and all the iron pipe were galvanized with zinc. Copper didn't seem to be abundant, however, present only in the thirty feet of old wiring.

"You are correct in assuming, though, that most of the metals are diffused through the soil of this area. These diffusions are not just at this location but cover a larger area."

"I was wondering if they might act as antenna of sorts to draw the negative energy that was causing the manifestations that disturbed Margie." I was trying to get around the "disturbances" question by specifying that Margie was disturbed, and perhaps I had, but I'd stepped into another hole.

"Realize," Elena said, "that the energies existing at this location are neither negative or positive. They are simply energies that exist, which may not be compatible with other energies. Yes, the metals here do act to draw and focus energies which are not compatible with the energies manifested through Margie."

"So the energies are not good or bad, but just are. And they bother Margie because they have, in a manner of speaking, a different polarity."

"This is correct."

"You mentioned other factors, such as a geophysical formation, that contribute to the overall effect. Would you please elucidate?"

"You are correct in your assumption that the geophysical formation is water. However, of greater effect is the electrical power plant."

How could I have been so thoughtless? A quarter of a mile down Margie's street was the electric company's transformer station that supplied the area with power. Talk about fire!

"This electrical plant," Elena went on, "causes an electromagnetic field which is drawn to the metals and which disrupts such energies as are manifested through Margie."

"You said before that the metals are in this general area. Are they more concentrated beneath this house?"

"The metals are distributed over a wide area, but there is a concentration of them beneath this structure."

"I'd like to know what correlation there is between the power spot in the therapy room, the mound of grayish earth directly beneath it, and the metal deposits."

"We know that you are aware of power spots. This particular spot is due to a concentration of energies directly beneath which are in a state of imbalance. These energies are trying to surface into the neutralizing condition of air and sunlight. The gray mound is as a pimple on the skin. It is a place where the energies are attempting to emerge and neutralize themselves, as when there are poisons in the body which the body works to the surface of the skin then out."

"Would it do any good to try to dig it out?"

"The metal deposits and energies that are emerging go down some eighty feet. To attempt to dig them out would only result in disrupting the energy's efforts to emerge and neutralize. It would merely emerge at another location."

"Okay, to get back to the geophysical formation," I said. "It is water, you said. Is it a spring or a stream?"

"The water is in the form of two flows which cross beneath this structure."

"Which ways do they run?" My original speculation had been that a stream ran beneath the therapy room, the main bathroom, and the living room.

"Realize they are not as you conceive. The two flows are at very different levels." With a start, I realized I'd been caught again. I had been thinking of them as being on the same level. "There is one which runs close to the surface which carries less water and is associated with a minor fault. It runs beneath the therapy room toward the northeast." That would be very similar in location to the one I'd envisioned. "The deeper flow runs to the southwest through this area, then changes direction toward the northwest. It runs much deeper than the other flow."

"So the shallower flow runs in the direction of the power plant," I said, realizing that it was the one directly affecting the apartment. "What effects do these streams have?"

"The shallower flow runs in the general direction of the power plant, through not directly beneath it. It serves to carry an electromagnetic charge toward this area from the power plant. The deeper flow does not carry a charge but causes a pooling effect in the earth deep beneath this area, which serves, along with the metal deposits, to intensify the electromagnetic fields in this location."

"So it is a combination of factors that are causing problems for Margie," I said, "The metal deposits and underground water serve to attract and channel electromagnetic fields to this place then intensify them. Further intensification was caused by the electric storm and rain."

"There are other factor which intensify the presence of electromagnetic energies," she said, "such as the proliferation in this area of domiciles and the electromagnetic fields associated with them and the presence of metal wastes. Realize that much of what man does upsets the balance of energies of the planet. All power plants, including nuclear power plants, that generate electricity, buildings and neighborhoods using large amounts of electricity, and high-power electrical lines have the effect of altering the earth's electromagnetic fields. Mining of metals and concentrations of nuclear waste also unbalance the energies of the planet. Millions of years have gone into achieving a balance that man has upset profoundly in less than a century. Modern man looks at the surface only, at the crust, and since he sees no obvious change, he thinks everything is the same, even when it is not."

Fascinating as all this was, I didn't want to keep Margie under for a long time, and I meant to stay to the point. I mentioned the miniature electrical storm that took place in the therapy room and asked if all the previously enumerated factors were responsible.

"There is a device which creates a negative electrical charge," Elena said, and I nodded, thinking of the negative ion generator that Margie kept turned on in the therapy room. "This created in the therapy room a condition of electrical vacuum which attracted the highly positive charges from the electrical power plant and the electric storm in the atmosphere."

"So she should remove the negative ion generator to avoid more lightning in the therapy room?"

"Due to the heat and dryness of the next few months, it is advisable that she operate it for short periods only or remove the device altogether." As it turned out, the dry heat that had characterized Houston's weather all summer so far continued, though fierce thunderstorms punctuated the dryness several times.

"Now I want to ask you about the ways this energy manifests toward Margie," I said. "What she experienced on Tuesday had strong overtones of terror, black magic, and evil. There were thoughts of the movie *Psycho*, the silhouetted head and shoulders of a man at the door, and the visions of the burning human flesh dripping blood and fat into the ground. Are these specific threats to Margie, or are they more like manifestations of generalized negativity towards her energy?"

"When Margie first moved into this apartment, she experienced an immediate drop in her vitality," Elena replied. "She attempted to rationalize away the loss, though the energies' presence continued to weaken her. These manifestations are the result of conflicting energies rather than being specific attacks. Realize, however, that the energies which are drawn to this location, being of their own specific nature, can only conflict with Margie's energies."

"Could energies that might be specifically or physically dangerous to Margie be drawn here? Could she be attacked?"

"This is possible."

"Since Margie's energies are at odds with the energies present in this location, your advice would be to move?"

"That would be advisable."

"At this time, Margie feels that financially she can't afford to move."

"We would remind Margie, as we have done before, that she is God. She controls the forces of her life, and if she does not move, it is because she, as God, has chosen to stay here. Man experiences himself as separate from Godhood, though this is not actually the case. We perceive that you, too, sometimes do not realize you are God."

"Sometimes!" I laughed. "I'd say it was more often than not."

Elena smiled. "We were trying to be kind."

"Well, back to Margie," I said. "When Margie does move, she should obviously avoid living near electrical power plants. What else should she avoid?"

"As long as Margie lives in an urban environment, she will encounter difficulties with electromagnetic energies. She should not live near high power lines, large buildings, or large metal pipes buried by other utilities. She also should avoid living by busy streets or highways, since motor vehicles in operation cause electromagnetic fluctuations in their immediate surroundings which would not be beneficial to her. Realize that Margie is highly susceptible to electromagnetism, which is what makes her a good channel."

"Since it may be some time before Margie chooses to move, I want to discuss ways to provide a buffer against these energies that may drain or attack her. Would it help, for example, for her to move her bedroom to the living room?"

"When Margie began working as well as living in her home, she increased the amount of time spent in conflict with the energies present. Since her work space and bedroom are together over the energy center, she is in almost constant contact with energies which are not beneficial to her. Though the energies do not manifest as strongly in her bedroom, the only exit from that room is through the therapy room. During the times of manifestation, she must pass directly through the center of disturbance. It is, therefore, advisable that she move her bedroom to the living room. This would bring about a relief from the constant and close conflict between energies now occurring."

"Would it help to have something physically present to help buffer her from the energies? Right now she has a bottle of holy water in the small hall between her bedroom and the therapy room. Would something like that help?"

"Such things are not in keeping with Margie's sense of being. We will not prescribe talismans, incantations, or cloves of garlic."

"Is there any other action she could take to buffer herself from the energies for the remainder of the time she feels she has to live here?"

"We cannot direct action or tell a person what to do."

"I see. I can ask questions that might have specific or general answers of an objective sort, but I can't ask what to do or what the future is."

"We cannot tell you what to do. However, asking about the future is a legitimate question."

I thought, "Do I want to know the future?" Then I thought, "No. Where's the fun in that?" Then I checked my watch. Margie had been in trance long enough. The future would have to wait.

"Well, I guess I've got the answers I need for the moment."

"If that is all, we will go."

"One more question, please. Your name?"

"Elena."

"Thank you, Elena."

"Thank you."

The session had lasted about half an hour. Margie's features went slack, and she sank back onto the pillows. She shivered for a few seconds then opened her eyes, which looked groggy and disoriented. She recovered after a few minutes, and I told her what had transpired. She decided to begin making plans to move, but in the interim, she would shift her bedroom to the living room. We talked a little more about the electrical plant and other aspects of the situation, then I left.

The next Tuesday, while at work in my office at home, I noticed that a thunderstorm was blowing in from the southeast. I thought of Margie and gave her a call to warn her of the approaching storm. She hadn't moved her bedroom yet, because she needed help carrying her bed and dresser. I volunteered and drove over to her house.

Luckily the storm proved to be mild, but even so, Margie was visibly depressed. She said she'd just gotten home a few minutes before I called and immediately felt her energy level decline. As we walked through the therapy room on our way to the bedroom to begin moving the furniture, we saw a curious sight. Margie's dog was lying directly on top of the power spot, as if to protect the apartment from its influence. I noticed that Margie had turned off the negative ion generator. Even so, I could readily feel the tingly electric sensation in the room. After Rafki moved from the power spot, I stood on it and again felt a strong current of energy passing through me.

Margie's energy level was obviously low that day, but by the following Friday she felt better. It helped, she said, to sleep in the living room, as far from the therapy room as she could get. In general, she felt more lively, and the therapy room and the former bedroom, which became her office, did not drain her as much during the time she spent in them. She speculated that the brightness of the living room during the day helped dissipate the energies. This agreed with Elena's statement that the energies were attempting to erupt into sunlight and air in order to neutralize themselves. That also might explain why one corner in the therapy room was less energetic than the general ambience, for next to it was the only section of wall in the room that received direct sunlight.

We went outside to practice tai chi, and I became aware of several interesting features of the backyard

I'd never noticed. First was the abundance of metal there. An iron stairway led up the outside wall behind Margie's back bedroom to the second story's back door, ending in an iron landing with iron rails. At the rear of the small yard sat an eight-by-ten-foot metal storage shed, and connected to the shed were four bare aluminum wires of a clothesline. The wires were about twenty feet long, and the other ends were attached to a standard clothesline T made of iron pipe that was planted about eight feet from the back of the house and the metal stairs. Finally, on the roof of the shed lay a very large coil of half-inch copper tubing that, unrolled, would have been fifty or sixty feet in length. I'd already found some of the iron and zinc deposits that Elena had mentioned beneath the house, and now I'd found some of the rest of it, along with a substantial amount of copper.

The power spot, iron stairs, clothesline with its attachment to the metal shed, and the copper tubing on top of the shed, were all within twenty-five feet of each other. The whole yard was like a giant antenna going twenty feet into the air and eighty feet into the earth. And all of it was directly linked, via the underground stream, to the nearby power station.

Less than two feet behind the metal shed, right on the rear property line, grew a largish oak tree with a curious feature. The tree's first forking occurred about a dozen feet above the ground, where the trunk separated into four major branches, each a foot or more in diameter. Just above the forking, however, the central two of the four major branches had grown back together and fused into a secondary trunk that went straight up several more feet before splitting into smaller branches. This odd growth pattern had created a natural doughnut in the tree trunk about three feet across with a hole in the middle about a foot in diameter. I'd never seen anything like it.

Margie then led me around to the front of the house and pointed out another feature. This was the presence of three electrical mains that emerged from the ground and ran up a telephone pole directly in front of the house. The mains were a second direct link to the power station. At the top of the pole, the mains, supported by heavy metal arms and brackets, split and ran in various directions to supply electricity to the immediate vicinity, With the presence of so much electricity and metal on the site, we marveled that more incidents hadn't occurred in and around the house.

There was one last interesting effect to be noted before Margie moved to a new apartment, which she did the next winter. I brought a pendulum over to her apartment, and we tried dowsing her energy and the energy of the power spot. When the pendulum was suspended over her right palm under normal conditions, the pendulum swung unhesitatingly clockwise. The power spot, however, caused the pendulum to swing strongly counterclockwise. When Margie stood on the spot and the pendulum was held over her right palm, it swung with the energy of the spot: counterclockwise. In other words, the power spot caused a reversal in Margie's energy flow.

A couple of weeks after the miniature electrical storm, I spoke to Rick Hawley, a friend who worked for Houston Lighting and Power Company (HL&P, now Reliant Energy), the city's principal electrical utility. I related the details concerning the electrical manifestations, and he nodded. He understood the mechanism behind the miniature electrical storm in the therapy room. In addition, he'd read a then-recent report on electromagnetic fields that surround high power lines and that are generated by power plants. The field around a power plant can have a radius of more than a mile, and in cross section, the fields surrounding high power lines take on a teardrop shape, with the tapered end pointing downward, the result of gravitational deformation of the field.

Power companies, including HL&P, have been sued for the purported negative health effects caused by high-power electric transmission lines. In 1985, HL&P lost one such suit brought against it by the Klein (Texas) Independent School District over the placement of 345,000-volt transmission lines that were run near three of the district's schools. Photographs were part of the evidence, and one, published on the front page of the *Houston Post* on November 28, 1985, showed two people standing beneath the power lines, holding four-foot florescent lighting tubes that glowed brightly, powered by current overflow from the overhead lines. Nicola Tesla, the electrical genius who invented the alternating-current dynamo, the electric motor, and, incidentally, the florescent light, used this wireless effect to illuminate his laboratory and astound visitors.

Many other such suits, however, have failed, often because scientific research—much of it generated by the power companies themselves—has not made a clear case for any negative effects that powerful currents and electromagnetic fields might have on living organisms.

But the simple fact is that the basic functioning of all nerves in all living things that have nerves is as much electrical/electromagnetic as it is biochemical in nature. Further, there is considerable reason to believe that the very life force itself—given many names such as chi, mana, prana, and so forth by different and separated cultures worldwide—has a strong electrical/electromagnetic component. And the flux and flow of many diurnal cycles are directly related to fluxes and flows in the Earth's electromagnetic field—a field whose effects now are being blanketed, scattered, and disrupted by multiple, human-made fields proliferating all over the planet. (See my book, *The Wellspring: An Inquiry into the Nature of Chi*, for a discussion of the bioelectromagnetic nature of chi and how it is produced in the human body.)

Mystics and seers of all times have viewed the Earth as a living being whose life manifests in weather, the tides, and fluctuations of the planet's magnetic currents. Indeed the Earth does seem alive. Tectonic plates move, mountains rise, flatlands stretch out. Far beneath the crust, the blazing iron core of the Earth whirls within its carapace of stone, spinning a web of protective magnetism that shields the planet from solar and cosmic radiation. On the surface, water flows, sands shift, and Life sprawls its panorama across many landscapes, all changing and all inextricably interconnected by overlapping energy fields.

Recent studies have pointed to a time, lost in prehistory, when human knowledge of telluric currents was widespread and possibly utilized for some specific purpose. Many ancient monuments, such as Stonehenge and the pyramids of Egypt and Central and

South America, are built with specific astronomical and terrestrial alignments, and studies of ley lines and the human-made features along them show that humans once were aware of forces that we seem to have forgotten—and that we have seriously dampened and disrupted since the advent of technology and the widespread use of electricity.

Today, humans are creating their own networks of currents, overlaying the natural rhythms of the Earth with an electrically generated patina that now adds vast wireless telecommunications networks to bands of frequencies already occupied by radio signals and television broadcasts. How do natural and mechanically induced energy networks affect humans? How will these energies affect each other as well as the future of the planet? Will they be opposing forces creating perpetual tension, or will they work together within a positive dynamic relationship?

These are a few of the questions humans will face as we learn more about telluric energies and mechanically generated electrical fields and their affects on each other and on life and humanity. Where we once saw limitless electrical power enveloping the planet, we need to realize that there might be a ceiling to safe use. But electricity has radically altered human life, and we're not about to abandon the benefits it has bestowed. As an HL&P spokesman put it after the judgment, "We're still in the electricity business, and we'll still be stringing lines."

It is toward an understanding of life, time, and space that intuition and intellect direct themselves. But the truth is, we know next to nothing about how our universe works aside from a few mechanical effects and a few "objective" measurements. And we know even less about the whys.

Searching for the hows and whys—for meaning—is our need as humans, as much as the tools of intellect and intuition are our birthrights. It is the same search that always has led to the conquering of old frontiers and the establishment of new ones. First, humans discovered new lands, then they colonized and mapped the globe. Now space, with its myriad worlds and mysteries, is the new physical frontier. Our nearest extraterrestrial neighbor, the Moon, is marked with its first few human steps and Mars with its first tire tracks. Two of our messengers—the *Voyager* spacecraft—have left the solar system on journeys that might take them to the far edge of eternity. And now humanity is at the point of tearing away from the nurturing parent of our species, the Earth.

It is possible that the development of a distinctly mechanical substitute for planetary electromagnetic fields may be a necessary precursor for our species as it prepares to travel extensively in space. Whatever the case, there seems to be evidence that, in the process of developing our own version of vibration generation, we should not forget the nurturing currents of the Earth.

Our entire civilization is in a constant state of agitation. Domiciles, neighborhoods, power plants, and whole cities are constructed without care for their relationships to one another, to the ground on which they are built, or to the sky into which they protrude. Modern man has practically no awareness of or regard for the energies of his planet. Perhaps it is no wonder. Constantly bombarded by high doses of every band of the electromagnetic spectrum and living in an envelope of psychic static, maybe we have lost a certain sensitivity to the planetary rhythms and currents around us.

But man has never been, it seems, without the ability to detect and map planetary currents. Builders of old have left us a wealth of such knowledge, even after millennia have passed. Rod and pendulum dowsing, Chinese feng-shui (geomancy), and other related arts can help reestablish our connections with our planet and, ultimately, with ourselves—connections we have lost behind an obstructing aura of human-generated electromagnetism.

Wise building with regard to natural currents of the Earth, electromagnetic and otherwise, could improve and enhance conditions in urban environments, releasing unnecessary stress from the tensions of escalating urban massing. The appurtenances of civilization could be located in spots conducive to the greatest effect and the greatest harmony for both the Earth and its inhabitants. As the gods, saints, and masters have told us often, our lives and well-being are in our own hands.

The Serpent and the Radiance

IT WAS THE LAST TIME that Julie and I tripped together—the last time that she took a psychedelic and almost my last experience. It was a balmy Saturday night in 1982, and we'd taken LSD late in the evening. We spent the next few hours sitting around, enjoying a fairly typical trip, until we went into the living room, turned the lights down low, put some music on the stereo, and began dancing.

We did not touch physically, but our dance became an intensely erotic co-mingling of our energy fields. There also was considerable psychic contact between us —a phenomenon we'd encountered often when taking psychedelics. The experience grew particularly significant after we put on the album *Remain in Light* by the Talking Heads. While we were dancing to it, I had my eyes closed, and after a short time, I found myself within a thick gray mist.

This mist didn't seem to be a figment of my imagination but a genuine, if psychic, reality. I had the impression that, for most people, myself included, our perceptions are so limited that they cannot penetrate the fog that masks deeper reality. With that thought, I felt a strong urge to go through the mist to see what was within it, to see if it had an end or another side.

I began moving through the mist, although this required an effort that was mental or psychic rather than physical. In fact, I was not really aware of my body, which I assume was still dancing, only of my mental perceptions. I had the feeling that I was not moving through the mist, exactly, but that I was, in a sense, forcefully pulling the mist around and past myself while I remained stationary. Another way to look at it was that I was willing the mist to dissipate from in front of me. The journey was not easy, as the mist proved a lot more substantial than mere fog, and movement was like pushing or swimming through a viscous liquid, although, again, the effort was mental, not physical.

After a short time, the mist ahead lightened. Suddenly, my head and torso burst through into clear space, and I beheld an astounding sight. I was looking at the inside of a tremendous tube that appeared to be many, many thousands of feet across. The space contained was so large that, initially, I was beset with vertigo. Several moments passed before I could adjust to the huge dimensions and begin to comprehend what I was seeing, and when I did, my reason was as shaken as my senses had been.

The mist through which I had come also formed the tube's inner wall, and at that interface, it was congealed into millions and millions of mostly faceless human forms. Some of the forms emerged from the mist wall only in shallow bas-relief, while others were nearly fully dimensional. Most were uniform in size, but some were larger to differing degrees, and the larger ones tended to be the most three-dimensional and to have discernible and individualized features. All of these forms were moving—gesturing, turning, bending, twisting, swaying—causing the inside wall of the tube to writhe and squirm as if alive.

I understood that the uniformly sized figures were humans, and the larger ones with faces were human archetypes and gods. And I realized with a shock that I was simply one of the smaller figures, surrounded on my side of the tube wall with other people moving, twisting, and gesturing. Unlike me, though, most of them did not seem to be aware of the tube but were caught by and lost in their own faceless personal identities and existences, blind to the vista of this ultra-reality opened before them. I also became aware that all of the writhing, moving figures were oriented with their heads in the same direction. This gave the tube an up and down, making it seem more like a well than like a pipe.

Realizing I was seeing something that always existed but that was rarely experienced consciously, I stared around the inside of the well near me then out across the gulf to the opposite side. The figures nearest me were my own size, those partway around the well were much smaller and like the faceless crowd at the far end of a football stadium, while those on the far side were so small that they blurred into writhing indistinctness. The only individuals clearly discernible over there were the larger figures that represented archetypes and gods, and they were huge giants in comparison to the small human figures.

I became specifically aware of two of the largest figures across the well, a bit to my right and somewhat below my level. They were Shiva and Shakti, who, in the pantheon of Hindu gods, create reality through the cosmic energy of their procreative dance. They were quite large in relation to the blurred, distance-reduced figures around them, and they were almost completely three-dimensional. But as large as they were, they were so far away that I could have blocked them from my sight with an outstretched hand.

I realized that Shiva and Shakti were dancing, as were Julie and I, in a dynamic, erotic interplay of cosmic energies that was at once procreative and completely nonsexual. And in the instant I understood that Julie and I were directly linked with their energies, Shiva and Shakti deliberately and purposefully looked right at me. Their eyes were a brilliant, burning red vibrant with energy, and they smiled wide as their thoughts—or should I say, a message—came to me, saying, "We are always aware of this reality, and we know that you can see us and that you are consciously, if only momentarily, experiencing the same interplay that we are." They seemed pleased by my awareness of them and our surroundings.

Then my eyes were drawn downward, deeper into the well—far below Shiva and Shakti, where even the largest of the figures blurred into distance. Just as water fills a well at its bottom, so this well was filled, though not with water. What I saw in the depths of this immense well was a tremendous, awesome, and completely conscious cosmic vitality. This vitality—too prodigious and powerful to be called an entity—was pitch black, but not with the blackness of shadow or empty space. Instead, it appeared to be a thick, dense liquid or jelly-like substance that gently pulsed, undulated, and quivered, its surface glistening with highlights.

The undulations, pulsations, and quivers sent waves and shivers of energy up the walls of the well, and it was those waves and shivers that vitalized the writhing shapes lining the walls. In fact, the writhing shapes were little more than ultra-complex ripples created in the substance of the dense mist by the movements of the black, liquid vitality. I and all the rest of the writhing forms comprising the inner wall of the tube were but temporary standing waves that would remain for but a moment or for many before sinking into the body of the mist. And just as water rises in waves and ripples then subsides on the body of the ocean, only to rise and subside again, so too did the waves of vitality produce newer and newer forms, but far more complexly. Creator of the well and motivator of the forms that lined it, the tremendous vitality below was aware of every aspect of the well and its inhabitants, but in a dispassionate way. Or more likely, its passion was completely beyond my ken.

For some indeterminate time, I observed the well, its inhabitants, and that which engendered it all, but too soon, the mist once again clouded my sight. I sank into it as a drowning man sinks beneath the waves, and I reemerged into my normal state of consciousness.

During all of this, Julie was having a very similar experience. She didn't push through a thick mist as I had, but instead, she just popped through, seemingly into the same tube of writhing, faceless human forms that I'd seen. She had the impression that the faceless, writhing forms were people waiting to be born.

For Julie, the tube's orientation was not up-and-down, as it was for me, but sideways. She began to fly down the tube toward one end, which opened into a vast space sparkling with brilliant lights like stars. As her vision opened up to take in more of what was in front of her, she realized that awesome and huge swirling masses of color similar to colorful images of galaxies and nebulae captured by the Hubble Space Telescope lay within the star-spangled space.

She, too, saw Shiva and Shakti: Their dancing bodies formed part of the vast, colorful backdrop. As she saw them, she realized that they were looking back at her, and she sensed that they had been waiting for her to see them, and she was surprised at their attention. Then, as abruptly as she'd emerged into the tube, she found herself back in her body.

The music was over, and tired, Julie and I sat on the sofa. We did not speak of what had happened then because we were struck speechless.

As I said, the air was balmy, and the window behind the sofa was open to the Houston night. By now, it was three or four in the morning. We sat there for several minutes, when Julie asked, "Do you hear that?" I listened in that unfocused way that one listens for sounds on the wind, and I realized that an incredible and glorious symphony of sound was permeating the atmosphere all around us.

Physically, the sound was not from a single, specific source such as a radio or stereo. In the same way that a musical symphony is an amalgam of all the instruments playing in concert, this was all the sounds of the city and environment combined—wind in the trees, traffic, air-craft at the nearby airport, a distant train, the rhythmic bark of a dog, faint music and voices, and more. Every sound that we could hear, including every sound that Julie and I made—even our own breathing and heart-beats—was part of the symphony. The manifestation was awesome and revelatory and not a little frightening in its power, depth, and pervasiveness.

The symphony was of such a homogeneity that most of the individual sounds were unidentifiable, though I could discern two distinct strains that quickly resolved into what may best be described as the inter-play between light and darkness, between good and evil, between that which seeks to rise and that which seeks to sink. And just as any great music elicits visual imagery, so did this, and what I saw seemed real and true rather than imaginary.

What I visualized was that the celestial symphony was produced by a shimmering celestial radiance that shot emanations of light into the night sky, while all around and through its luminous core entwined a sin-uous, twisting, coiling blackness. The whole was like a dark serpent slowly writhing around in a patch of tall golden wheat, and the writhing blackness was what caused the shafts of radiance to shimmer and shine, just as a serpent's movements would cause the stalks of golden wheat to shake and waver in the sunlight.

It was the shimmering of these celestial strings that produced the symphony. Of the few individual sounds that I could pick out that composed these two aspects of the symphony, a choir seemed to be a major com-ponent of the radiance, and appropriately, the song

"Highway to Hell" by the band AC-DC was one of the elements of the serpent.

Significantly, this interaction between the light and the darkness did not manifest as a contest or battle between the two but as an interplay. Although certainly, in one aspect, it was the conflict between good and evil, it was less the Christian concept of an eternal struggle for dominion between God and Satan than the Taoist idea of equal but opposite forces that at all times mutually oppose one another but that also mutually create reality through their interactions.

Without the serpent, the radiance would be an undifferentiated glow with no movement or direction to reach in; without the radiance, the serpent would be undifferentiated darkness with no manipulative ability; and without their collaboration, there would be no reality, for it is the shimmering waves of energy created by their relationship that cause reality to manifest. Perhaps the shimmering shafts of reality that I was now seeing from the outside were, from the inside, tremendous wells writhing and rippling with waves of reality-creating energy. Shiva and Shakti, whom Julie and I had just met, were a major intersection of these basic contradictory forces, just as, on a smaller scale, Julie and I had been in our dance, just as, at every moment, we all are within reality and within ourselves. Dancing with life.

At last the symphony faded—not because it was no longer there, but because we could no longer perceive it. All that remained were the sounds of our daily lives playing like solo instruments whose musicians wear sound-proof headphones.

I am interested in the differences in Julie's and my perceptions of the experience. We each experienced our orientation to the writing tube differently—sideways for her, up-and-down for me—and we each saw a different manifestation at the end of the tube—massive, colorful, swirling galaxies, nebulae, and stars for her, and a shimmering, quivering dark mass for me.

The orientation matter is the simpler of the two. Throughout, I remained "attached" to the wall of the tube, and when I saw the writing forms making up the wall were aligned roughly in one direction, I naturally adjusted my perception so that all the heads were "up" and feet were "down." That induced me to look downward, toward the shimmering, quivering darkness that created the waves of energy rippling up the tube.

Julie, on the other hand, emerged into the space inside the tube and so developed no particular orientation to the writing wall. Also, the wall did not hold her attention for long because she began flying down the tube toward the cosmic vision she saw at its opening.

As for the differences in what we each saw at the end of the tube, were those due to individual interpretations of the same thing, or were we each looking in opposite directions: she toward one end and I toward the other? Did I see the being—or process—that creates the manifestations, and she the vast creation of manifestations? I might not ever know—at least in this lifetime—but could I only hear them, Shiva and Shakti might have the answer.

Cosmic Wheels

THE BURNET INCIDENT IS DIFFICULT to talk about. In part this is because the experience took place under the influence of psilocybin mushrooms and thus has an implausibility factor high enough to cause many critics to dismiss what happened as pure fantasy at best or group psychosis at worst. In fact, psychedelics do not generally deliver wholesale fabrication or cause a person under their influence to see or experience anything that does not have some basis in reality. However, that reality may be a little more expanded and intense than the user normally experiences—or bargains for—and sometimes it's even out of the realm of the tangible and rational.

But psychedelics, if they do nothing else, make it obvious that reality has a much broader spectrum of operation than most people can apprehend in the conventional state of their lives. It can be said that psychedelic "hallucinations" are amplifications of perceptions or, alternately, a stripping away of barriers that prevent us from perceiving a broader range of the larger spectrum of reality. This is precisely the reason that psychoactive drugs have been employed for millennia by mystics and shamans the world over. But none of these reasons, nor the fact that five of us underwent the same experience, will silence critics.

So be it. A man who has seen the ocean does not let a man who has dwelled only in the desert convince him that such a large body of water cannot exist.

The incident is difficult to talk about also because so much of the experience was internal. Perhaps I should say that it is difficult to convey. Describe to me, for example, what joy feels like, or hate or puzzlement. Descriptions of these states would be largely impossible—and certainly unintelligible—if we were not able to use our shared humanness as a referent, resorting to something like, "You know what I mean."

To further illustrate—try to explain empathy to a psychopath or color to a sightless person. Happily, most of us do share perceptions and understandings of common emotional and mental states such as joy, hate, and puzzlement. And this same sort of understanding extends to psychedelics, at least among those who have taken them. The problem with the psychedelic experience is that it is not a universal human sensation but an induced state, and I can resort to "You know what I mean" only with someone who has experienced that state and does know what I mean. As Jimi Hendrix put it, "Are you experienced? Have you ever been experienced? Well, I have."

The other four who experienced the Burnet incident do know what I mean, especially with regard to this particular encounter. Like me, they were caught up in and connected to what was happening, and we each played a part. But as individuals, we perceived the experience from our own perspectives, and we responded differently.

We are now somewhat separated by time and circumstance, and it is unlikely that I would be able to obtain written documentation from one of the people involved describing her personal memories of what happened—or her understandings and beliefs about what occurred. And it would be impossible for another, who has since died. But I have talked extensively with the other two, and we agree on much of what we think about what happened. I've asked them to write down their recollections, and those follow my account.

It was 1978, and for the past year, I'd been living in a big, ramshackle house near Rice University in Houston, Texas, working as a printer, and engaged in producing the first issue of my first literary magazine, *Phosphene*. After I'd lived alone in the house for a few months, my good friend, Charles, moved in, and not long after, I met and began dating Julie, who eventually became my wife. A couple of months later, Charles' friend, Carl, also moved in. Carl's girlfriend, Katy, spent a lot of time at the house, too.

Charles' parents lived on a small ranch outside of Burnet, Texas, a small town a little more than an hour's drive northwest of Austin, and early in November, they told him they were going out of town over a long Thanksgiving weekend. They said we were welcome to stay at the ranch while they were gone, so the five of us decided to drive up there.

Early on the morning before we left, we visited a certain area of mixed forest and prairie near Addicks Dam in west Houston. Today, this land is surrounded by subdivisions, shopping centers, and schools, but it remains much as it was then because it serves as a detention reservoir for flood waters that otherwise would more frequently inundate Houston than they do. In 1978, though, development hadn't reached this far, and this area was just beyond the edge of the city.

The land's primary use, when it wasn't flooded, was as cattle pasture, but it had another function known to some in the counterculture—a function related to its use as a pasture, because out of the cow dung grew abundant and very potent psilocybin mushrooms. Unfortunately, as knowledge of the area's special crop became more widespread, so did the number of harvesters, and the next few years saw the fields picked clean. But everything has its time and life span, and subsequent development of the surrounding subdivisions and widening of roads made access difficult, so perhaps it is just as well that the fields are no longer productive. Or, I assume they aren't—I haven't been to them in many years, and I sometimes wonder if magic mushrooms still grow there.

With a sack of mushrooms, we returned to the house, packed Charles' van, and left for Burnet. It was about a five-hour drive, and when we arrived, Charles's parents already were gone. We chose our bedrooms, ate dinner, hung out for a while, then went to bed.

The next day, about midmorning, we consumed the mushrooms. Each of us ate four to seven mushrooms and drank a large cup of mushroom tea—a pretty hefty dose. We sat around the house until we began to feel the effects of the psilocybin, at which time, Charles suggested that we go outside and walk around.

The ranch was nearly rectangular and about a hundred and sixty acres. If you were to divide the property along its long, east–west axis, the north half lay atop a flat rise, and the south half sloped gently into a long, shallow valley. The dirt road that led to the house and the unoccupied land beyond ran just outside the north fence line, and the house was situated near the back of the northeast quadrant. Most of the ranch was covered in scanty, knee-high grass with a liberal scattering of various sorts of cactus and scrub brush, and small- to medium-size trees—mostly oaks—grew in clusters or copses in the fields, around the periphery, and at the back of the southern half. At the time, there were no domestic animals on the ranch, though Charles' parents later raised goats, horses, and lots of cats and dogs.

The November day was cool, overcast, and gray, with enough misty humidity in the air to threaten a light drizzle. Charles led us to a tank—a small, shallow pond designed to hold run-off rainwater for livestock use—that lay in the middle of the north section of the property, a hundred and fifty to two hundred yards from the house. Small rushes grew from the tank's mucky bottom, but the piled earthen rim was bare and dry.

We sat on the rim or stood around watching the bugs and small frogs in the rushes for a time, then we grouped in a clearing in the grass nearby as we discussed what to do next.

I use the word "discussed" loosely, because by now the psilocybin had taken firm hold and we were tripping, so our talk was fairly disjointed and indecisive. It didn't really matter what we did since there weren't a lot of choices: We could stay there, we could walk around, or we could go back to the house.

As we stood there, shifting around in the clearing, Charles said, "Do you feel that?"

I don't think any of us really heard him when he first said it, but he repeated the words several times more insistently, and as he did, he swayed oddly to and fro.

After a minute, Julie said, "I can feel it. I can feel it." And she swayed, too.

That got my attention. Something was going on, and I looked to see what it was. And as soon as I paid attention to their movements and to sensations in my own body, I felt it, too. And suddenly, I could "see" it, as well.

To explain this "seeing," let me refer to those three-dimensional pictures that are printed in various places, such as newspaper supplements. When you first look at one, it is just a repetitive abstract pattern. Not until you learn to focus your eyes properly—or unfocus them properly, that is—does the three dimensional image hidden in the abstract pattern pop out. In this case, seeing what Charles and Julie were referring to required a more generalized perception rather than specifically focused attention.

What I perceived was that the five of us, grouped in a rough circle, were connected to each other by an elastic field of energy. When one of us moved, everyone moved. It was as if we were standing with a large rubber band wrapped waist-high around our circle, and when one person pulled back or stepped forward, the rubber band would tighten or slack off and create or release tension on the others in the circle, making them move. I could see the energy field as a sort of shimmering, shifting net that encircled us but also that connected each of us to the others with lines of force woven around, between, and among us. The lines of force were strongest and most apparent around our middles and seemed to emanate from there.

"I can feel it, too," I said, and I deliberately pulled the elastic net one way then another to demonstrate. Everyone moved, and Charles and Julie laughed.

"I don't know what you're talking about," said Katy. "I don't feel anything." Carl said he couldn't feel anything, either. Even though they'd both move within the force field when one of the other of us moved, and we moved when they did, they couldn't perceive it.

Or said they couldn't. Later, Carl admitted that he could feel it, too, but since Katy said she couldn't, he didn't want to make her feel left out or embarrassed that she was unable to perceive it. And much later—years later—Katy told Charles that she had felt the force, but she'd said she couldn't because she was frightened. In retrospect, this isn't surprising since Katy was a strong proponent of the highly rational—if you couldn't quantify it, it didn't exist. And here we were, faced with something that was obviously un-quantifiable and irrational, yet very real.

Charles, Julie, and I played with the elastic feeling for a few more minutes, but then Katy, with a touch of anger, said she still couldn't feel anything and that she was going back to the house. She left, and Carl, with a parting comment that we were nuts, went with her.

We were a bit unsettled by our friends' abrupt and slightly acrimonious departure. Some time went by after they disappeared inside the house—maybe five minutes, maybe twenty—and Charles, Julie, and I could still feel the force surrounding us, though it was diminished and less interesting to play with now that two of the energizing bodies were absent.

As those minutes passed, Charles began to feel agitated, and the agitation soon grew to near-panic. He said he felt sick and had to go back to the house. He started to walk toward the house, then abruptly, he started running. Julie and I, who felt no panic or nausea, looked questioningly at each other and followed Charles at a walking pace.

Parallel to the dirt road that ran just outside the north fence was the electric power line for properties along the road. The ranch's supply line split off the main line and angled two to three hundred feet across the property to the house. I hadn't really paid much attention to it since power lines are ubiquitous in the modern world. But out here, this was the only electric line for miles in any direction.

As Charles sped full tilt toward the house, Julie and I witnessed a most peculiar sight. When he ran beneath the power line, it was as if he slammed into a rubber wall. One second, he was running, and the next, he rebounded and was flung backwards through the air several feet. He staggered back a little farther, fell, and lay there on his back, unmoving.

Equally amazed and worried, Julie and I ran toward him. When we reached him, we saw that he was conscious.

"Are you all right?" I asked.

With mumbled, almost incoherent words, Charles indicated that he wasn't hurt but that he wasn't all right, either.

I asked if he wanted us to help him up and get him to the house, but he said he didn't think he could stand or walk and just wanted to lie there for a while.

Julie and I stood near, watching over him. After a couple of minutes, I heard him mumble something else.

I stepped forward and leaned close, but though audibly louder, the mumble was no more comprehensible than before. I could make out fragmented, rapidly spoken words, but nothing seemed connected or to make any sense. Otherwise, Charles seemed okay, so I stepped back.

As my distance from him increased, the mumbling diminished in volume, which was to be expected. But oddly, though I now could barely hear it with my ears, the mumbling seemed more distinct and intelligible. Wanting to know what Charles was saying because it suddenly seemed important, I stepped up and leaned close so that I could hear more clearly. But again, as the mumbling grew audibly louder, it lost all coherency. One thing was plain, however: The vocalizations had grown in magnitude, amplitude, and intensity and were now delivering a rapid outpouring of images and ideas.

I stepped back, and as the audible volume decreased, the distinctness and coherency returned.

Something strange was going on here, and it rang a bell. About a month before, Charles, Carl, and I had tripped at our house—this time on LSD—and at one point during the evening, Charles started mumbling in much the same manner as he was now. The mumbling didn't seem to be conscious speech on Charles' part, but rather as if his stream of consciousness was attempting to vocalize itself. But his state did not have the earmarks of a trance, either. Instead, he appeared to be completely awake and aware, though not exactly in control.

Carl, who'd been sitting next to him on the sofa, kept asking "What?" and leaning forward to hear better. I, too, leaned forward but could not hear, much less understand, what Charles was mumbling, so I eventually stopped trying. Nor was Carl able to glean any meaning, despite his attempts to do so.

Now, looking down at Charles lying in the grass, I realized that if I wanted to comprehend what he was saying, I would have to ignore what I was hearing with my ears and "listen" to him in a different way, just as I'd had to "see" in a different way to perceive the shimmering elastic force that had connected us.

While the mumbling continued, instead of stepping forward and trying to hear it with my ears, I stepped back and just listened, as if I was seining distant sounds on the wind. And as I listened, the mumbling suddenly became intelligible, if no less a stream —a flood—of consciousness in which I could recognize and comprehend images and ideas but never grasp or retain them because of their volume, depth, intensity, and speed.

The astonishing thing was that I was hearing this stream of consciousness within my mind, not with my ears. The reason the images and ideas had seemed indistinct and fragmented before was that I had been trying to hear, capture, and process them—to rationalize them. But the images and ideas were rushing too rapidly for rational analysis. Comprehension, in this state, required that I simply let them flow through my own mind, and when I did, I could take in their overall meaning—or at least some of it. The flood was no less than a mass of information about the nature of humanity and reality.

As I listened, I became aware of a couple of things. First, the stream of consciousness was not coming from Charles, per se, but rather was flowing through him from another source. And second, it was rapidly increasing in force. Over the span of a few minutes, it grew into a great fountain of primordial information so intense and powerful that, although I beheld the whole, I could absorb and integrate only a small portion of the peripheral spray.

With my seeing that wasn't sight, I could see the fountain visibly gushing out of Charles' abdominal region. It looked like a cylindrical, dense gray geyser that began about two feet in diameter and shot fifty or sixty feet into the air, where it spread out enough to disperse into the gray atmosphere. The psychic pressure of the fountain translated into a physical energy that made Charles repeatedly thrust his pelvis off the ground in a movement that looked sexual though not erotic.

I quickly learned that moving farther away heightened the telepathic link. I stepped back, and as I did, I realized that more was happening. I began to perceive the thoughts of Charles as an individual distinct and separate from the primordial fountain emerging through him, and I became aware of Julie's thoughts, as well.

Rather than being fountains, the human thoughts were like abstract, organic cityscapes, with taller, partially or completely luminous towers of the more conscious thoughts and personality characteristics rising from a lower, subtly glowing mass of unconsciousness. I could hear in my mind the whole of their thoughts, though only the more prominent spires came across as clear, coherent expressions amid the subdued murmur of their minds' unconscious workings.

I wondered if they were as aware of me telepathically as I was of them. Since Charles was incapacitated and profoundly preoccupied, I focused on Julie's thoughts and called with my mind, "Julie!" Instantly, she looked up at me, and I could feel her mind reply, not with words but with a question that asked why I'd called her. "Just checking," I thought, and understanding beamed back from her.

Because Charles was in distress, I moved in close, bent over him, and asked how he was. I could tell he was in great discomfort, but I also knew, for some unexplained reason, that he was not in danger. In fact, it seemed more dangerous to try to halt the energy fountaining out of him—through him—and move him than it was to let him lie there and allow the experience play out. So, there was little left to do but to explore the experience.

The energy in the air was incredibly intense, and it was beginning to affect Julie and me in a new way. I'm not sure exactly how it started, but soon, Julie began walking in a circle around Charles, at a radius of eight or ten feet. Every two or three steps, she would make stylized postures, gesturing out to her sides with her arms, sometimes palms up, sometimes out, sort of like a halting, angular modern dance. A corona sparked off her hair, and each time she gestured, bolts of energy almost like lightning—though I don't think they were electric—discharged out of her fingers into the surrounding air. I had the distinct impression that Julie was acting as a transmitting antenna, broadcasting signals from the fountain gushing from Charles out into the atmosphere.

Wanting to hear the telepathic resonance better, I moved farther away and let go of my conscious control over myself. Before I knew what was happening, I was dancing around Charles and Julie in a curving path that spiraled outward until I was walking in a circle about seventy feet away from Charles. It was as if he was a sun and Julie and I were planets orbiting around him.

My dance was a sort of combination of walk, stalk, and gyration, and inside, I was caught up in an enchanted, boundless ecstasy of understanding and oneness with creation. I had taken psychedelics many times during the preceding decade and had many instances of telepathy, psychic connection, and intimations of profound cosmic understanding and universal harmony and oneness, but never with this depth or power or on this scale. This time, it was not a haphazard set of perceptions and impressions but as if a prodigious intelligence was personally and purposefully informing and directing us.

In this state, I orbited across the ground around my friends for many circuits before I realized that my eyes had been closed almost the entire time I'd been dancing. I was astonished because, even with my eyes closed, I could see everything around me, though in a different way than with my eyes. All color was gone, and everything was grayish. I could see the ground and plants, I could perceive Julie and Charles not as people but as organic mental cityscapes, and I observed the lightning and sparks flashing from Julie's cityscape and the primordial fountain of information gushing from Charles' center.

While all this was going on, I was of two minds: On the one hand, if I let go of myself, I was gripped by the experience and totally controlled by it; on the other hand, my participation was completely voluntary, and at no time did I lose cognizance of who and where I was. And though I might not have known what actually was happening—and I certainly had no control over the experience itself—I discovered that I could emerge from the experience any time I wanted and regain personal volition then reinsert myself into the experience, also at will. I did this many times throughout the experience to survey the safety of our surroundings and to check on Charles to make sure he was okay.

I also investigated the validity of the several apparent psychic phenomenon that were occurring, such as being able to see without using my eyes. Once I realized that I was seeing psychically, I deliberately held my eyes shut yet still could see the surroundings I moved through. This ability to see was as clear as my normal vision at close ranges, but it grew hazier the farther away I tried to look, much as if I was looking through a light but far-reaching fog. The house, five hundred feet or so away, was about the clear limit of my inner sight, and the valley beyond was pretty misty looking. With my eyes open, I could easily see well past the house to the valley, with only a trace of fogginess due to the damp air.

During the experience, I tended to keep my eyes closed. Not only was it more relaxed and natural feeling, it seemed to strengthen the telepathic connection with the other participants and my link to the power that was fountaining through Charles and causing us to move like we were. I suppose it is a testament to the reality of my blind vision that I spun and gyrated around that field for quite a while with my eyes closed, yet never once bumped into any of the abundant cactus or other jagged plants growing there.

I also reverified the telepathic contact I had with both Charles and Julie. I called their names in my mind, and each time I did, I heard a mental response. Julie would turn and look at me, and while Charles couldn't react physically, I could hear his response in my mind and see his mental cityscape flare.

We remained this way—Charles at the center, geysering primordial information, Julie orbiting around him at close range and transmitting information, and me orbiting some seventy feet away—for an indeterminate length of time. It seemed timeless and eternal. It could have been half an hour, but I think it was closer to two or more hours because it began to fade only after the effects of the psilocybin began to wane, which should have occurred no sooner than four hours after we first went out into the field. Also, by the time it was over, we were quite physically worn out.

However long the experience lasted, it was long enough for me to experiment with my state. As I said, I retained complete volition, even while being gripped by the experience, and I tried various things besides emerging to check on Charles and our general welfare.

I wondered about my orbit and varied its radius. If I got too close in, my perception of the voice of the primordial fountain grew too physically aural, and I could no longer comprehend it. If I loosened the orbit and spun too far outward, the telepathic connection became extremely tenuous, and I would hear Charles and Julie's voices in my head saying things like, "You're too far away" and "Come back," urging me to return to my, it seemed, ordained orbit. After some experimentation, I discovered that I had a ten- to fifteen-foot allowable variance in my radius, which averaged, as I said, about seventy feet.

I also quickly noticed a peculiarity of the electrical line—the same one under which Charles had seemed to have slammed into and rebounded from an invisible elastic barrier. As I danced in my orbit around Charles, I passed beneath it twice during each circuit.

For me, it was not an impenetrable barrier as it had been to Charles, but I could feel the electromagnetic field surrounding the line as a disruptive, penetrating vibration that gave off an unpleasantly nasty buzzing feeling and disturbing hum. Each time I passed through this field, I felt resistance, as if the air was thicker, and while I was on the other side of it, the telepathic connection with my friends would be dampened. The electromagnetic field's disruptive influence was strongest beneath the line, but it extended fifteen or so feet on either side.

What I noticed most, though, was a copse of trees not far from us—about sixty feet out from the southeast quadrant of my orbit, on the opposite side of my orbit from the electric line. The copse consisted of five or six youngish oak trees and was thirty or so feet in diameter at its base. Interestingly enough, the copse was shaped like a giant mushroom, and beneath the misty, lowering skies, it had a shadowy, fungal appearance. After repeatedly passing the copse during my orbit, I realized that it was occupied by a powerful consciousness—an entity—that appeared to be the source of our collective experience.

The copse was not the entity, nor did it seem that the entity was always there. Instead, the entity was using the copse as a temporary residence or anchor. My initial impression was that the entity was a manifestation of— or caused or summoned by—the mushrooms. Just as those who take peyote often report meeting a supernatural being that *is* Peyote, the entity in the trees may have been a personification of psilocybin mushrooms. It might also be significant that the trees of the copse were oaks. Oak trees and copses were thought by the Druids to contain spiritual entities and also are known for sheltering "fairy rings"—circular growths of mushrooms— beneath their boughs.

Whatever the entity was and wherever it came from, it was clearly the intelligence and power behind what was happening. I believe that its being suffused us, linking us and causing us to move, and that the geyser of information fountaining through Charles was its voice or thoughts communicating with us.

Despite Charles' discomfort, the entity was very enchanting, friendly, and even jolly. It seemed to delight in engaging us, much like an adult delights in playing with a young child and showing it new wonders. I can't pretend to have understood its motives—maybe I did at the time, but if so, that sort of cosmic information left me when the experience ended and the drug wore off. I'd taken mushrooms a number of times before and have since and never had any other intimation of this being. But I, as well as many others, recognize that the psychedelic state of mushroom intoxication, while similar to that of LSD, is warmer and more personable.

Maybe the particular configuration of people present and in a psychedelic state had, so to speak, opened a portal through which this entity manifested itself to us. There were, after all, originally five of us standing in the field, creating the net of shimmering energy. Standing in a circle, we formed a rough pentangle—the standard configuration occultists use to summon otherworldly beings. In fact, the lines of energy that encircled the five of us and ran directly between us did form, together, a pentagram surrounded by a pentagon, which itself was encased in the circular force field. Perhaps the candles at the corners of the occultist's pentangle should not be taken literally but are symbolic of humans "lit-up" on psychedelics.

It might be that the entity deliberately grouped us together in this way to show itself to us and instruct us. I believe it also is likely that our location, where external electromagnetic interference so prevalent in cities and towns was at a minimum, played a part.

That the entity might have been imaginary is an idea I totally and unequivocally reject. All five of us felt the experience, and the three of us who participated in the ritual dance all agree that we were in complete telepathic contact throughout and that the entity was present in the copse of trees and controlling our actions. Interestingly enough, the entity referred to itself as the Human Organism.

Charles geysered and Julie and I danced, and although Charles was uncomfortable, for me the experience was exhilarating, incredibly uplifting, and awe inspiring. I was shown that energies do truly link us all, at many levels, and I later came to understand that the energy net we saw must be what the Chinese call chi. The principal lines of energy were all connected to our waists, which I've learned is the seat of the tantien— the area approximately behind the navel where a person's chi is generated and stored.

I'd had enough previous paranormal experiences to know that reality is populated by various types of entities who are non-corporeal to those of us on this plane of existence. But my prior personal experiences had been with lower-level entities, some even mischievous or harmful. Now, I was allowed personal contact with one who was far more powerful than I could have imagined, and by treating us to its humor and compassion, as well as to its knowledge, it made me unafraid, though I suppose it could have wreaked havoc upon us.

In the end, the knowledge it imparted was, for the most part, lost on such small and simple human organisms as us, but three important lessons remained for me. First, psychic energies do, indeed, tangibly connect us all. Second, there is an entire spectrum of "supernatural" beings that most humans cannot perceive, from the base to the great, which can directly affect us under the right circumstances and conditions. And third, humor, goodwill, and acceptance can allay fear, even in the face of incredible mystery and power, transforming the mystery of life and reality into some form of understanding, and transforming fear of the power into a yearning to be at once greater and more whole.

I suppose that each of us took something away from the experience, though I often regret that two of us succumbed to their fear. All during the cosmic dance, Carl and Katy huddled in the house, feeling the experience and, to some extent, gripped by it, but too frightened to come out and be fully engaged.

Perhaps with good cause. I speculate that, had they participated, our group would have been incredibly powerful but that the experience may well have been detrimental to us as individuals because of our very human weaknesses. The reason is that Charles' heaving and thrusting had a certain sexual nature. Both Charles and I believe that Carl was intended to take an orbit farther out than mine—much farther out, perhaps a mile or more. And I further believe that Katy would have gravitated to Charles and sexually ridden him, amplifying, focusing, and channeling the energy rushing through him.

But Carl and Katy did not participate, and our group's full power and abilities, whatever they might have become, were not realized. At last, the experience waned as the effects of the psilocybin weakened and the physical strain began to tell on all of us. My rational mind understood that we were becoming exhausted and had to stop, so I pulled myself out of the grip of the experience and spiraled in toward Charles and Julie. By now, Charles was simply lying there, heaving only slightly, and as Julie and I mentally backed out of the experience, he finally lay quietly. Eventually, we helped him up and got him to the house, where Carl and Katy said they were glad we'd broken off the experience and come inside.

Afterward, we all sat around in the living room, not saying much and trying to calm the experience and restore the normal order of things. But even if we were ready to stop, the experience hadn't quite let go of us. Every once in a while, one of us would loosen up and again be gripped by it, which would set all of us in motion, and we had to forcibly resist to end it.

One of these moments helped convince me utterly that the experience was real. Leaving the others in the living room, I went into the bathroom to urinate. When I was done, I stood there and, thinking myself in a private place and unobserved, let the experience take me over once more. I swayed to the internal rhythms, closed my eyes, and saw the bathroom in the hazy gray light. Instantly and simultaneously, all four of the others yelled from the living room, "Stop it!"

I stopped.

Julie's account of the experience:

In 1978, five friends decided to take psilocybin mushrooms together. The mushrooms had previously been
gathered from rural pasturelands west of Houston, at
spots known to those who took them. My boyfriend,
now husband, Chris; his two roommates, Charles and
Carl; Carl's girlfriend, Katy; and I were eager to leave
the city for a weekend trip to Charles' parents' ranch
in rural Burnet County. With his parents conveniently
out of town, we would have uninhibited access to
their grounds.

This part of Texas has a landscape of sparse trees
and vegetation with dry earth and rocky terrain, which
makes for clear visibility. Also, we thought that being
out where there were few inhabitants and interference
from city static and electromagnetic fields would make
the mushroom trip more enjoyable.

When we arrived, we sat and talked and relaxed as
the mushroom tea steeped. Once we drank it, we decided to take a leisurely walk out onto the property to
explore. It was a tranquil day. As we walked, the five of
us came on to the mushrooms. We stopped at a place
out in the middle of the property. As the drug en-
gulfed me, this part of the property became an area
overlooking an abyss. For me, the daylight faded to
night. This night was spectacular with a clear, star-
studded view of a brightly lit moon. We were scattered
about but could see and hear each other with a kind of
extrasensory perception, making us fully aware of each
other intrinsically.

At some point, I noticed that Charles had squatted on
the ground. I could see thick cords of light and electricity

emanate from his midsection, spew into the air, and then seek to connect to each of us. I was closest to him, and as the cords attached to me, I heard a humming sound. They then traveled to Chris and connected to him. Then I watched the cords reach towards Carl and Katy, but as they neared them, the cords lashed about unattached.

I sensed fear from Carl and Katy and tried to communicate to them telepathically to let it happen, to participate. Instead, the two of them intransigently turned to leave the area. I could see the lines of communication dissipate as they retreated. The cords that seemingly were meant for Carl and Katy whipped back then reattached to Charles with an energy that further lit his body with an additional charge, causing him to reel back and lay on the ground.

Charles was so enraptured that he appeared as a white light. I could see that whatever was causing this to happen had fully inhabited his consciousness. I stayed near him out of concern that he wouldn't be able to endure it. I could hear him exuding what I deemed to be universal knowledge. The closer I got, the more I could hear. A voice, not his own, was speaking to me through him! It was a benevolent voice, clear and calm, that I didn't hear with my ears but with my whole being.

My attention was diverted to a clump of trees in the distance, where I saw a mass hovering in and around it. This mass, an entity, was delivering a message to Charles, the receiver, who then delivered it to me, the antenna. Then the cords connected to Chris illuminated as I delivered the message to him. He was like a satellite, farther out, orbiting in a circular motion.

He became like Mercury, the messenger, who was waiting to take the message farther out into the universe. If he moved too far away, I thought the message wasn't being transmitted at the right frequency and produced static. When he stayed within range, it was unbroken from Charles to me to him.

The entity seemed to control the message and made clear that its purpose was to deliver this message to all receptors—those who were properly attuned. The message was both a warning and an instruction to respect the Earth and all that live on it. It spoke of higher beings and a complexity of the universe that humans could sense only under the right circumstances. It was a benevolent being who wanted us to feel, hear, and know this truth.

Charles' account of the experience:

Four friends—Chris, Julie, Carl, and Katy—and I collected psilocybin mushrooms from the pastures west of Houston, and went to Burnet, Texas, to do them. This was desirable to get away from all the electromagnetic fields of the city, which tend to distort the psychedelic experience. We ate the mushrooms and waited for them to take effect.

We began walking out into the fields away from the house where we were staying. We moved as if we were a pack, and each person had a role and a position. Chris and I had experienced this many times with various people while walking the streets of Houston at night under similar conditions. I was usually at the center, as was Chris.

Once out in the field, I began channeling energy. This, too, had happened many times before, but this time it was more practiced, as were our pack movements. It felt like a river of light, a fountain that was flowing through me from foot to head then shooting up in the air and spreading out from there, connecting to everyone else. We were all enveloped in what seemed to be the cell wall of a single, collective organism, with streams of bright energy connecting each of the others to me. As I moved, the cell moved with me, and the other four revolved around me as if I was the sun and they were the rest of the solar system.

Each of the others circled me at various distances, some a few yards away, some a few dozen yards away. Ropes of energy connected us. I found that if I focused, I could control the individuals and even have my thoughts come out of their mouths. It was as if we had become a single organism. Another entity was using me, channeling through me, and I no longer felt in complete control.

While three of us—Julie, Chris, and I—moved in harmony, Carl was unable to accept what was going on. I realized that, although he had been with Chris and me on previous trips, for him, doing psychedelics was just a way of getting mentally drunk. He'd always fall into his self-absorbed Catholic concepts, and this experience was too alien to the Catholic mythology he had grown up with and never thought much about for him to accept. For him, there had to be good and evil, saints and sinners, and a Catholic panoply of angels and demons.

As he stood near me, with the others orbiting beyond, he began to address me and the force I was channeling. His questions were about Cain and Abel, and it was as if he was saying that it would kill one of us to acknowledge what was happening. I was unable to speak because of the force of the energy rushing through me, so I responded by having Julie drift over to answer his questions.

Carl's girlfriend, Katy, could clearly feel and see that all this was happening, but she wanted to reinforce her boyfriend, so she denied what was going on, as well. I engaged her in dialogue about the reality of the experience, and although she denied that I could speak through different mouths, the debate continued to come at her from three directions: Julie, Chris, and me. Her denials, it seemed, were not based on her experience or beliefs but on her support for Carl.

All this got to be too much for the two of them, and they decided to go back to the house. They went that way, and Julie, Chris, and I started to follow, but as we passed under the electric line that ran to the house across the fields, I fell to the ground. My right side was paralyzed, and all I could do for a period of time was grovel on the ground. Julie and Chris started to rotate around me at various distances.

As I lay on the ground, I began to realize that while I could not move in space, I could move through time. I began to do so, watching the trees around me come and go. Since this was an entirely natural landscape, I could not tell anything about the changing of time except that the vegetation would change. I did not know whether I was going forward or backward in time, but now I realize that there were no buildings, roads, or fences, and there are more today than there were in the past, so I must have been going backwards in time.

As I flew through time, I found that I also could project myself through space. It was as if I would see the ground from the air, and I was connected to my body by a long tunnel. If I strayed too far, I could send a message to Chris and Julie, who were still circling me, and they would talk me back to my body where it lay on the ground.

I also realized that, over a long period of time, Chris and I had developed these abilities to move across the landscape as if we were a single-celled organism. The ability to do this came from many experimental trips during which we deliberately developed tools and abilities without actually talking about doing so. Instead, we tended to discuss the experience and effects.

In the city, however, the experience was always distorted by electromagnetic fields emanating from a variety of human-made sources. Electrical wiring, large masses of metal, and so forth had prevented us from unfolding the organism's shape fully, and even planes flying overhead would cause distortions in our fields.

We were not anticipating that the organism would form when we went to Burnet. During the experience, the shape was more fully developed than we'd ever had it, but even here it was warped by the power line, which also had the effect of paralyzing me.

In the end, I cannot say whether it was a force field or an intelligent being. During the experience, I kept saying, "The Organism will be complete," and at times, it seemed we had become parts of a single-celled organism. There was an emotional energy that was not coming from me, and it felt like Chris and I, after many experiences doing these trips, had unleashed something that I could not control. But it was controlled.

Many years later, I was housesitting in the Tidewater Country on a neck of land that had formerly been a plantation owned by the proprietor of a slave market. The house faced a creek not far from Chesapeake Bay. A friend was visiting me, and we sat on the porch and looked out over the fields at the creek and the bay. As we sat on the porch, we felt a force come over the house: The porch wood creaked, the walls creaked. I didn't like it, so I pushed it back. It felt exactly like I was at the center of a cell, and I could push the malevolent force back. It emanated from a small wetland that drained into the creek before us.

Time after time this happened, and without me saying anything, my friend said, "I feel something evil coming over us." Then, as I pushed it back, he would say, "Now its receding." We did this many times until finally I revealed that it was me that was pushing it back. To prove it, I stopped pushing, and when it came back, many boards creaked. I let it flow over us until my friend said, "You can push it back now."

I later learned that there had once been a house by the creek, and tragedies befell the family that lived there. They all died young, and at least one was a suicide.

Afterword

MUCH AS HUMANS MIGHT LIKE to live a less stressful and more fulfilled life, that's a goal nearly impossible to accomplish. Reality not only is dangerous, it also is implacable in its requirements and startlingly short in duration. And on top of that, it is as deeply frightening as it is mysterious. We've spent millennia eking out the barest of knowledge about the vast and often hostile universe— visible, invisible, and non-visible—within which we live, yet we are really no closer than ever to understanding the least bit about what's actually going on. We pretend otherwise, but we know only a very tiny amount about very little, and even that little isn't durable and will vanish in time. And in fact, it might not even be real. Are we a con- struct of matter? A flux of energy? A hologram? Maybe we're simply a vague thought in the mind of something much vaster than we can conceive of or a momentary flare of in-consequential fireworks in a night sky. And where did the matter come from? The energy? Who or what made the hologram, dreamed the dream, or lit the Roman candle?

We can say only this: We are. Even if we aren't.

In other words, we can meditate all day long on whether Zhuang-zi's dream was one of a human imagining he was a butterfly or of a butterfly imagining he was a human, but very likely, pain from an injury would immediately anchor most of us back in the here-and-now. So the here-and-now—our reality—is what we initially have to work with and what necessarily must underlie forays into the unknown.

As one might imagine from the stories told in this book, I am a believer in seeking to penetrate the veil of mystery to see what lies beneath, above, or beside reality; to understand what makes reality tick; and to give my puny, violent, greedy, insane monkey brain every chance possible to make some sense of the awesomeness of creation spread infinitely and eternally around and through me. I do not consider myself a psychic detective or ghost hunter who wants to record and study paranormal phenomena, nor a psychonaut who deliberately delves into psychic depths in search of.... Well, probably in search of many things. Or of One thing.

What I am, in a sense, is an accidental tourist. Follow- ing the overall pattern of my life, I am just a person who has witnessed many interesting incidents and had many compelling experiences, not because I sought them out, but because I just happened to be there and was open to possibilities within reality that aren't always obvious or even immediately apparent. I was "there," just like I "am." But I deeply appreciate how a grounding in mysticism has helped me accept and make sense of the many experiences in my life that were more extraordinary than the usual sort of historical event. I feel the same way, ironically, about science, which is another system, though at odds with mysticism, whose purpose is to make sense, through consensus, of our mysterious reality.

Here is not the place for the Science versus Mysticism debate. Both systems have their depths and limits, their successes as well as failures. Science can have a great positive impact on mysticism by helping demystify certain aspects that were mysterious only because their true nature was not yet known. But despite what many scientists believe, science cannot explain everything or supersede mysticism because science, by its very nature, explores and codifies the immanent world and cannot speak with any accuracy or authority about those aspects of reality that cannot be quantified. Observe the current befuddlement over Dark Energy and Dark Matter.

I will jump in here, though, with my thoughts on one pet theory of modern brain science: that one can dismiss mystical states and paranormal experiences as merely by-products of quirky bioelectrical activity of the brain. This is an explanation that explains nothing. Nor does the fact that mystical states can be induced by artificial stimulation of the brain prove that mystical and paranormal experiences can be relegated to the status of brain states. This line of reasoning mistakenly conflates function—or worse, mechanism—with purpose.

Another way to put it is that I can drive to a lecture on some philosophical topic, and later, I can drive to the store to buy a loaf of bread. The purposes of neither is to induce the electrical and mechanical effects of my car. Nor are my actions or purposes manifestations caused by the operations of my car's electrical and mechanical systems. Instead, I have purposes that transcend my vehicle, and even the two purposes are quite different in nature. One is task driven and caused by a tangible and basic physical need—to satisfy my hunger—while the other is event driven and has the more esoteric intellectual/emotional purpose of communicating and receiving abstract information that does not necessarily positively impact my physical well-being.

In addition, I could drive my car around at the direction of a passenger, thus exhibiting very few connections between my car's systems and my personal purposes, mental attitude, or state. And despite my passenger's apparent control of my car's movement, he or she has no actual physical connection to my car's systems much less to my own state of being.

Yes, brain activity takes place when a person is in a mystical state, just as my car's systems activate when I drive. Certainly it does. But the activity is a container, not the contents, a manifestation of the mechanism, not the cause of the manifestation, much less its purpose.

The truth is, it is not the method of stimulation—natural inclination, meditation, drugs, injury, disease, or probing—that is important, but the subjective impact on the individual engaged in the experience. And that can't be measured directly because there aren't yet instruments that can measure, for example, the soul. We can't even measure love or hate except in the abstract, though few people would deny their existence. In fact, even words often prove inadequate when describing mental, emotional, and spiritual content, partly because we don't always have referents for such experiences in our cultural make-up and partly because words can't fully convey the inner impact of such experiences. As the eighteenth-century Scottish philosopher, Thomas Reid, put it, "There is no greater impediment to knowledge than the ambiguity of words." But if everything else is relative, how can words be otherwise?

However, although I criticize science for its often-resistant mind-set, it certainly has made life on this plane of existence deeper and more interesting. I deeply appreciate the many medical advancements that have prevented me from being a blind cripple, for example, and while I might hold mechanically generated electromagnetic fields suspect in terms of human health and well- being, I do love electric lighting, my refrigerator, and my computer. The best thing about science is the tools it has developed to assist us poor humans in figuring out how reality works and what it is all about. I like to use those tools to pare away the dross—not to debunk but to allow me to more sharply focus on the many legitimate aspects of mysticism and the paranormal.

And even where science might have shown me a physical mechanism behind a so-called paranormal aspect of life, it often hasn't erased the mystery but simply enhanced techniques that further empower the mystery. For example, my scientific examination of the life force the Chinese call chi, resulted in my uncovering the mechanism by which chi is produced in the human body, how that energy can be directed within the body, and how it can extend to interact with reality. It also helped give me practical tools—certain exercises—to strengthen and manipulate my personal chi field. What my research couldn't answer, though, among a host of other questions, was what sorts of things and events are produced, say, by interactions of large-scale fields. Nor could it re- veal the reasons that the universe's interacting fields exist in the first place or how they operate.

My interests lie primarily in trying to draw connections or parallels between the many disparate experiences I've had and non-corporeal entities I've encountered. This is not always easy, but a couple of strains have become apparent. The first is that there are a number—perhaps a great number—of types of non-corporeal entities that interact, to some degree, on or with our earthly plane of existence. Many of these entities cannot be readily perceived, while others are more obvious. Some seem benign, or even actively helpful, while others are destructive or corrupt. Are they angels and demons? Maybe, but they also behave pretty much like a cross-section of humanity.

Another strain is that reality is like a liquid substance that exists in multiple dimensions and that can be excited by waveforms and vibrations from bodies that generate magnetic and electromagnetic fields. The infinite interactions of literally countless waveforms are what create the many structures within the substance of reality. Even science agrees with this when it says that everything in our tangible environment consists of nothing but vibrating atoms whose constituent "parts"—subatomic particles—can currently be observed only by inference. Everything is a pattern of energy—mysterious energy—projected upon a ground state formed of the same energy in quiescence.

It seems clear that these waveforms and vibrations of energy are transmitted in all frequencies and in all "directions" through a multilayered complex of dimensions, and that a material object is like a cluster of vibrations with a unified "frequency" or "resonance" that is distinct from other frequencies. This difference in vibratory rates is what separates individual objects—both animate and inanimate—from one another. As signals extend their waveform spheres into infinity, their effects disperse and diminish to become, with distance or dimensional angle of approach, just more of the background field—the palpable gray mist—that forms the body of reality.

Further, if life on Earth is a representative example of life elsewhere, living beings exhibit behavior that inanimate matter does not: Inanimate matter, once created, immediately begins to succumb to entropy, while animate matter exhibits syntropy, for a while at least, by accrual of mass and energy, by growing and developing, and by structuring their environment, often to suit the expansion of their form of life.

The questions remain, as they always do: What is the base substance of reality composed of, and who or what is broadcasting all the waves? Is there one root source, or is everything just random fluctuations in a base energy field caused by infinite, spontaneous broadcast sources? What makes animate matter arise from inanimate existence? And now we can wonder about a new unknown: the identity of Dark Energy and Dark Matter.

For us on Earth, a more practical consideration is what effects the plethora of our artificial signals might have on our own energy makeup. The vibrations of the many biological bodies, devices, and celestial bodies that produce magnetic or electromagnetic fields will impact, to a greater or lesser degree, other fields within their effective range and, therefore, must be affecting our own fields if we are in range. It's a matter of physics. Currently, those interactions are often beyond our ken and manifest in ways we can't always readily perceive, but nevertheless, they can deeply affect us and our lives.

Some of these waveforms might be of immense pow- er and able to act like a huge ripples in a pond that affect every molecule of water they wash through. Think of a tremendous electromagnetic field whose waveform's vibrational rate either dampens or amplifies human- generated fields, perhaps inciting humans to violence or soothing them to artificial tranquility. Recently, an article in *Popular Science* (http://www.pop-sci.com/article/technology/mysterious-phony-cell-towers-could-be-intercepting-your-calls) reported on the existence of eighteen cell-phone towers around the Washington, D.C., area whose owners and operators are unknown and that don't transmit normal cell-phone signals.

Whether or not this claim is valid is, at this time, in question, but if these towers do exist, the speculation is that they are used to surreptitiously gather cell-phone data from phones pass- ing within their range, either for economic gain or espionage. However, it also could be possible that someone is using them to broadcast signals to deliberately influence people passing within their range. That might not be the purpose of these particular towers, but almost certainly someone will eventually try mass cultural engineering by manipulating human biofields with external signals.

This possibility underscores the more benign idea that the expanding and overlapping fields of the universe, by their very nature, have the potential to carry information to those who are in tune with them. Precognition and telepathy seem, to me, to be two interlinked elements within this strain, but perhaps the fields can carry various sorts of influences that can affect us, positively or negatively, like a breath of fresh air or a flu epidemic. Or COVID-19.

At the very least, the sheer number and strength of artificial signals must form a sort of constant static that would tend to cut people off from the energies of the cosmos and do much to separate them from one another on a psychic level. No wonder humanity is currently fractured and suffering from wounds that won't heal. Planet-wide, we are dealing with our own intolerance, closed-mindedness, and lack of meaningful communication as we isolate ourselves from one another and then fear and hate the strangers we find ourselves among.

The stories in this book relate most of the major un- usual or paranormal events in my life, but such things happen to me all the time on a smaller scale. I've had interesting experiences with psychics of different sorts, Smiley and the Captain still visit, and synchronicity and other odd events continue to play strong roles in the reality presented to me. I can't say I'm sorry. A pinch of serendipity, a dash of footsteps in the dark, and the breath of a mysterious voice stirring on the wind make a heady recipe for life. And when all is said and done, I can't help but hope that my last mystical experience on Earth will be the best of all.

Phosphene Publishing Company publishes books and DVDs related to literature, drama, history, Texana, film, the paranormal, spirituality, and the martial arts.

For other great titles, visit
phosphenepublishing.com